CULTURES OF THE WORLD
Libya

Cavendish
Square
New York

Published in 2016 by Cavendish Square Publishing, LLC
243 5th Avenue, Suite 136, New York, NY 10016
Copyright © 2016 by Cavendish Square Publishing, LLC

Third Edition

This publication represents the opinions and views of the author based on his or her personal experience, knowledge, and research. The information in this book serves as a general guide only. The author and publisher have used their best efforts in preparing this book and disclaim liability rising directly or indirectly from the use and application of this book.

CPSIA Compliance Information: Batch #CW16CSQ
All websites were available and accurate when this book was sent to press.

Library of Congress Cataloging-in-Publication Data

Malcolm, Peter, 1937- author.
Libya / Peter Malcolm, Elie Loslenben, Yong Jui Lin, Charles Piddock and Debbie Nevins.
pages cm — (Cultures of the world)
Includes bibliographical references and index.
ISBN 978-1-5026-0798-0 (hardcover) ISBN 978-1-5026-0799-7 (ebook)
1. Libya—Juvenile literature. I. Loslenben, Elie, author. II. Yong, Jui Lin, author. III. Piddock, Charles, author.
IV. Nevins, Debbie, author. V. Title. VI. Series: Cultures of the world.

DT215.M3 2016
961.2—dc23

2015035324

Writers, Peter Malcolm, Elie Loslenben, Yong Jui Lin; Charles Piddock, third edition
Editorial Director, third edition: David McNamara
Editor, third edition: Debbie Nevins
Art Director, third edition: Jeffrey Talbot
Designer, third edition: Jessica Nevins
Production Manager, third edition: Jennifer Ryder-Talbot
Cover Picture Researcher: Stephanie Flecha
Picture Researcher, third edition: Jessica Nevins

PICTURE CREDITS

PRECEDING PAGE

The marketplace at the ruins of Leptis Magna near Al Khums, Libya

Printed in the United States of America

CONTENTS

LIBYA TODAY

L **IFE GOES ON, AS BEST IT CAN, BUT LIBYA TODAY IS NOT A HAPPY** place. Four years after the October 2011 overthrow of Libyan dictator Muammar Gaddafi, mounting chaos has gripped the North African country. Libya now has two opposing would-be governments, parliaments, and armed supporters. Prime Minister Abdullah al-Thinni's government is based in Tobruk with its own House of Representatives. Acting Prime Minister Khalifa Al-Ghweil's government controls Tripoli. The two are fighting each other in Benghazi, the Sidra oil basin, and other parts of the country. In the midst of this civil war are ever-changing "micro conflicts" featuring tribes and towns and militias large and small, all with different and frequently shifting allegiances and grievances.

In other parts of Libya, the terrorist groups Al Qaeda and Ansar al-Sharia, are vying for power. To make matters worse, the dreaded black flag of ISIS, or the Islamic State, the armed Islamist group that has already taken over large parts of Syria and Iraq, has been raised in Libya and is gaining territory.

Nearly two years after the September 11, 2012, attack on the US consulate and CIA outpost in Benghazi, Libya, Islamist fighters took control of the US embassy

Buildings in Derna, Libya, are destroyed after Egypt bombed the neighborhood in February 2015, in an attempt to stop the militant group ISIS.

in Tripoli, Libya's capital, after all embassy personnel had been evacuated to the neighboring country of Tunisia. On May 27, 2014, the US government advised all US citizens in Libya to leave the country immediately and advised all US travelers to avoid Libya. By mid-2015, most other foreign embassies, offices of the United Nations, the International Committee of the Red Cross, and other international agencies withdrew their staff and closed their missions in Libya. Armed groups also attacked, threatened, assaulted, or arbitrarily detained journalists, judges, activists, politicians, and ordinary citizens with impunity. Lack of protection for the judiciary resulted in a near breakdown of policing and justice in Tripoli, Benghazi, Sirte, Sebha, and Derna.

By mid-August 2015, most of the city of Sirte, the hometown of Gaddafi, had fallen to ISIS, which had recently made advances across the country. In the past year, ISIS has set up checkpoints and established its presence in places across Libya. The militant group has taken over the Libyan city of Derna, a city of 100,000 on the Mediterranean coast. Evidence shows ISIS militants in Libya killing two groups of mainly Egyptian and Ethiopian Christians.

At the end of August 2015, warring factions continued to shell civilian areas in both Benghazi and Tripoli, seized people, and looted, burned, and otherwise destroyed civilian property. Benghazi remains a war zone, where fighters loyal to both governments, as well as ISIS and other jihadist groups, battle daily. Large parts of the city have been destroyed and hundreds of civilians have died in the fighting.

During this time, militias, mostly from Misrata, continued to prevent about 40,000 residents of Tawergha, Tomina, and Karareem from returning to their homes as a form of collective punishment for crimes allegedly committed by some Tawergha residents during the 2011 revolution that overthrew Gaddafi. Those who were displaced continued to seek safety and shelter in makeshift camps and private housing in many areas, but they remained subject to attack, harassment, and arrest by the militias. So far, Libyan authorities have failed to end the attacks or hold those responsible to account.

Armed factions threatened and assaulted dozens of journalists and attacked several media outlets, including private television stations. Several journalists and an activist were abducted or seized. Six journalists were assassinated.

Fighters from the Libya Dawn militia secured the perimeter of the Mellitah Oil and Gas Terminal in Zwara, Libya.

The fighting has also devastated Libya's economy. Although Libya has the largest oil reserves in Africa, and the fourth largest in the world, its oil industry is barely functioning. With nearly all of Libya's oil fields and terminals attacked or closed, the country is producing an estimated 160,000 barrels of oil per day, down from its post-Gaddafi peak of 1.5 million barrels a day. Libya now imports around 75 percent of its fuel for domestic use. Chronic cash shortages, unpaid government salaries, electricity cuts, and soaring gasoline and food prices are producing miserable living conditions for Libyans. The country's economy actually *dropped* by over 24 percent in 2014, chiefly due to the civil war and the decline in the world price of oil.

Caught in the middle of this bloody chaos are Libya's 6.4 million people. By July 2015, around 400,000 Libyans found themselves homeless refugees, including about 100,000 residents of Tripoli. Another 150,000 people, including foreigners, had fled the country. A record number of migrants and asylum seekers embarked on the perilous sea journey from Libya to Europe, with 60,000 reaching Italy alone in 2014. The Italian navy's large-scale rescue operation, *Mare Nostrum*, rescued around 100,000 from un-seaworthy boats, but at least 3,000 still perished at sea. By the end of August 2015, the refugees fleeing by sea from Libya turned into a flood. On August 22, Italy's

Migrants from
Libya arrive in
Tunisia following
their rescue by
the Tunisian
coast guard in
June 2015.

coastguard rescued about 3,000 migrants after receiving distress calls from more than twenty overcrowded vessels drifting in the waters off Libya. At least another thousand rescued migrants were headed for Italian ports on other boats.

The flood of migrants by boat from Libya and by land through Turkey has caused a major crisis throughout Europe. Thousands are trying to escape into Hungary, Germany, Italy, and then to Great Britain. Alarmed governments have fortified their borders and have attempted to put the migrants into camps. By early September 2015, riots erupted, especially in Hungary, as the migrants resisted being shipped off to refugee camps.

Not all the migrants fleeing Libya by sea, of course, are Libyans. Some come from other countries in Africa, the Middle East, especially war-torn Syria, and South Asia. But all are affected by the anarchy and chaos in Libya and pay money to unscrupulous and dishonest Libyan boat owners to escape to Europe. In 2014, just over 170,000 migrants landed at Italy's southern ports after being rescued. The total for 2015 in Italy topped 104,000 by mid-August alone. A further 135,000 have landed in Greece since January 2015. More than 2,300 have died at sea. Many of the rescued migrants tell of vessels packed with more than ten times the number of people the vessel was designed for, with many of the passengers, including women and children, locked below decks.

The United Nations envoy to Libya, Bernardino Leon, warned in July 2015 at another round of attempted peace talks between Libya's two "official" governments that the country was really "at the limit" and that Libya was on the verge of becoming a "failed state." Bankruptcy beckoned and within six weeks, he warned, the rival governments wouldn't have enough cash to pay the salaries of public workers, including their fighters.

Rupert Colville, spokesperson for the UN High Commissioner for Human Rights, denounces the atrocities of ISIS.

In August 2015, Boko Haram, an Islamist militant group from Nigeria, sent two hundred heavily armed groups to help ISIS in Libya. ISIS is fighting in Libya because it believes the country is a launch pad to its conquest of southern Europe, and also because the country's instability makes it an easy target. ISIS is suspected of planning to stow away fighters on smugglers' boats full of migrants headed for Italy and Greece.

After an imam in Sirte called for people to resist ISIS in August, he was promptly killed. ISIS insurgents then staged summary executions in Sirte, brutally killing a number of people in a horrifying public display. Rupert Colville, the spokesperson for the Office of the United Nations High Commissioner for Human Rights, said, "It seems that the public flaunting of these murders is intended to send a message to anyone challenging [ISIS] in Libya."

The hopeful time that followed Gaddafi's ouster has now disintegrated into chaos. In Libya, hard times will surely continue, but to what end?

GEOGRAPHY

A camel passes by a sand dune in the Libyan Desert.

1

GEOGRAPHY HAS SHAPED LIBYA with an iron hand. The great Sahara Desert has determined the way people live and use the land as well as age-old customs and ways of life. Along the Mediterranean Coast, the sea has spurred the rise of great cities and trade with the rest of the world. Under the desert's barren sand and stones lies a treasure trove of petroleum—the remains of plants and animals that lived in the region thousands of years ago when it was not a desert, but a lush tropical grassland.

Libya is located at the center of the north coast of Africa. Tunisia and Algeria lie to the west, Niger and Chad to the south, and Egypt and Sudan to the east. Libya's 679,362 square miles (1,759,547 square kilometers) make it the fourth-largest country in Africa, one-fifth the size of the United States and just larger than the state of Alaska. Over 90 percent of Libya is desert, with rain falling only once every two to three years.

Over two-thirds of Libyans live on two narrow coastal strips near the Mediterranean Sea. Farther south there are scattered oasis settlements in the desert—a bare, dry world of sand and rock interrupted in places by pipelines. When the stretches of desert are included, Libya's average population density is only 5 people per square mile

A nomad carries his belongings on three camels.

(3 people per sq km). Population density is about 130 people per square mile (50 people per sq km) in the two northern regions of Tripolitania and Cyrenaica, but falls to fewer than 2.6 people per square mile (1 person per sq km) elsewhere. Ninety percent of the people live in less than 10 percent of the area, primarily along the coast.

Libyans of the desert have developed a way of life that allows them to survive in a harsh world. Their most precious possessions are animals—camels, sheep, and goats—and their survival depends on the availability of water.

Families adopt a nomadic lifestyle, constantly on the move to find water holes and fresh grazing land for their herds. Unfortunately the unpredictable nature of the desert means that a water hole might be overflowing in one season and might go dry the next, so families never settle anywhere permanently.

THREE MAIN REGIONS

Libya has three main regions: Tripolitania, Cyrenaica, and Fezzan. Until 1963 these regional names were the official names of provinces, but now they just indicate general geographic areas.

Tripolitania is Greek for "land of the three cities," in reference to Sabratha, Leptis Magna, and Oea (Tripoli). Its size is 110,000 square miles (284,900 sq km), and it has a low, sandy coast that is occasionally fringed by lagoons. On the coastal Al-Jifarah Plain are salty marshes, sand dunes, and stretches of coarse grass, where wheat and barley are planted between rocky olive groves, together with fruit, cauliflower, tomatoes, and almonds.

The city of Tripoli as seen from the air

The city of Tripoli has been the capital of Libya since its independence in 1951 from Italy. It has been a fast-growing city, with new high-rise apartment buildings steadily taking the place of single-floor dwellings and improvised shanties. Palm trees and ornamental gardens fringe the Mediterranean shore, but any untended ground is hard and dusty.

Behind the coastal area, the land rises in a series of steps to the limestone ridge of Jabal Nafusah, which reaches a height of 2,500 feet (762 meters) in some places. Old craters and lava rocks indicate its volcanic origin. On the southern slopes, some figs and barley are grown, but the countryside is too dry to support much life. The area has been significant since before recorded history as a major population and cultural center of the Berber people, and it still shelters most of Libya's Berber-speaking population. On the bare, red sandstone plateau of Al Hamra' in northwestern Libya, desert nomads keep small herds of sheep and goats. In some places, attempts have been made to "pin down" the drifting sand with squared patterns of tough, rooted grass, and to plant species of fodder shrubs that can survive in dry areas. To the east of this region are the Black Mountains, an unyielding wilderness of sharp, black basalt rock.

Cyrenaica (350,000 square miles, or 906,500 sq km), Libya's other fertile coastal strip, has the towns of Benghazi and Tobruk. This area was once Greek, and the ruins of ancient Cyrene still attract visitors. Cyrenaica was the center of the Libyan anti-Gaddafi forces in the 2011 Libyan civil war, with the National Transitional Council based in the city of Benghazi.

Inland the limestone plateau of the Green Mountains (Jabal Akhdar) reaches a height of 3,000 feet (914 m) in two slender strips, each only a few miles wide. When in season, the mountains are covered with a carpet of lilies, anemones, cyclamen, and narcissus. The higher parts have thick, thorny scrub, and there are patchy remains of juniper forests. Lotus grows in some of the damper southern valleys. The region is one of the very few forested areas of Libya, which is one of the least forested countries on Earth. It is the wettest part of Libya, receiving some 24 inches (60 centimeters) of precipitation annually. The high rainfall contributes to the area's large forests. It is an area that enjoys rich fruit, potato, and cereal agriculture, something of a rarity in the arid country.

The Green Mountains (Jabal Al Akhdar) rise near Benghazi.

Not all of the Sahara is sand. In fact, sand dunes cover only about a quarter of the 5.7 million square miles (9.1 million sq km) of the Sahara, the second-largest desert in the world, after Antarctica. Much of the Sahara is covered by rock and gravel. Its highest parts are the Tassili N'ajjer in Algeria and the Tibesti Mountains, both touching the

southern borders of Libya. Surrounding these mountains are plains of gravel formed partly from ancient riverbeds. Stretching from the Atlantic Ocean to the Red Sea, the Sahara contains mountains that reach up to 11,204 feet (3,415 m) in height; lost oases; forgotten cities; salt, iron, copper, and uranium mines; oil wells; and plains of multicolored rock, gravel, and sand.

THE LIBYAN DESERT

To the south of the Green Mountains lie the sweeping sand dunes and stony plateaus of the Libyan Desert, a part of the greater Sahara Desert. This arid region extends to southwestern Egypt and northwestern Sudan. Little can survive on these windswept, sunbaked plains of gravel. The temperature is seldom below 40 degrees Fahrenheit (4 degrees Celsius) and frequently above 100°F (38°C). There are scattered settlements, mostly oases with a few thousand inhabitants. Stores of underground water have been discovered at Al-Kufrah, allowing agriculture. For centuries, artesian wells in the Fayyum Oasis have permitted extensive cultivation in an irrigated area that extends over 811 square miles (2,100 sq km).

The bulk of the southern part of Libya is loosely known as Fezzan (270,270 square miles, or 700,000 sq km), although this name actually

Umm al-Maa (the Mother of Water), a freshwater lake, creates an unexpected oasis in the Ubari Sand Sea.

applies only to a depression about 300 miles (480 km) south of Tripoli. Located in the Fezzan are two of the larger oasis settlements, Sabha and Murzuq. This is harsh desert country where life depends on springs and wells fed by underground water.

In more recent times, the Fezzan saw many traders traveling between the Phoenician—Roman coast and the rich areas of central Africa. Today, occasional camel caravans still thread their way across wastelands of sand, from oasis to oasis, as they have done for centuries. One of the five ancient north—south routes goes through Sabha, where the path diverges to go southeast and southwest. A fort stands on a flat-topped hill some distance from Sabha. It once housed a French garrison but is now a police post. Most of Fezzan is flat, but a section of the Tibesti Mountains, mostly within Chad, Bikku Bitti, rises on the border to 7,440 feet (2,267 m)—the highest point in Libya. Three "sand seas," which contain dunes up to 1,680 feet (512 m) in height, cover approximately one-quarter of the region.

The northern shores of Africa, including the Nile Valley, were the grain-producing areas of the Roman Empire. In Libya, more than two hundred Roman wells have been discovered. Once cleaned, they work as well as they did two thousand years ago. The Roman settlers and farmers dammed up narrow dry valleys known

as wadis to trap moisture. Aqueducts 70 to 100 miles (110 to 160 km) long, shown here, were built to carry water to the public baths in the thriving coastal cities.

CLIMATE

Within Libya five different climatic zones have been recognized, but the dominant climatic influences are Mediterranean and Saharan. Most of the country has a desert climate, with an average annual rainfall of only 10 inches (25 centimeters), which falls intermittently between November and early May.

Around the cities of Tripoli and Benghazi, the rainfall may reach 14 inches (36 cm) a year, but the desert areas (94 percent of the country) receive less than 4 inches (10 cm). Deficiency in rainfall is reflected in an absence of permanent rivers or streams, and the approximately twenty perennial lakes are brackish or salty.

Sabha, the main town of Fezzan, has been called the driest town in the world. Even in areas close to the Mediterranean, the summers are viciously dry and hot. Average winter temperatures vary from 52°F to 63°F (11°C to 17°C).

A sandstorm in the desert makes seeing and breathing almost impossible.

Summer temperatures range from a low of 82°F (28°C) to a high of 100°F (38°C), but can rise to around 120°F (49°C). A world record of 136.4°F (58°C) was recorded in 1922 at Al Aziziyah, only 50 miles (80 km) southwest of Tripoli.

There are areas in the Libyan Desert where children grow to the age of ten years or more without ever having experienced rain. Such areas are called the sand seas because there are no shrubs or stones, only sand. Sandstorms called *ghibli* (GIB-lee) sweep across the desert two or three times a year in what seems like a wall of wind and red sand up to 2,000 feet (610 m) high. The winds can raise the temperature by as much as 20°F (7°C) in a few hours, causing severe damage to crops. Along with the storms come a parching dryness and sand that clogs eyes, nose, and ears.

The winters can be bitterly cold and unpleasant. Frost—sometimes even sleet and snow—is common in the mountains, and the desert nights are chilling. The winter rains along the coast of the Gulf of Sirte can turn limestone dust from the surrounding desert into seas of mud that make travel slow or almost impossible.

The high inland ranges receive only an inch or two of light winter rain each year. This is enough for the scattered spiny shrubs to survive, providing grazing land for the hardy sheep and goats of many nomadic groups.

There are no permanent rivers anywhere in Libya. If a rainstorm does occur, the streams that flow downhill to the valleys are soon lost in the dry earth. Droughts that last one to two years occur every five or six years.

WHAT LIVES IN THIS LAND?

In this dry climate, grass grows where it can. Esparto grass was once Libya's main export crop. It was used to make fine paper and rope. Herbs grow near the sea, including the asphodel lily, which the Greeks associated with death and planted on graves. Wild pistachios and henna shrubs that make a

THE PALM TREE

In Libya, palm trees are found either by the sea or by most oases. It is never too hot or cold for the date palm, which survives night frosts and even snow. Date palms are either male or female. Pollen from a male tree is necessary for a female tree to produce fruit. The Bedouin believe palms that grow close together are friends. If one dies, the other trees will droop in mourning.

Nomads use every part of the date palm. The trunk provides timber, fuel, and fiber to make sacks and rope; the stalks are used for fences and roofs; the stringy part of the leaf is woven into baskets, mats, and sandals; and the juice of the young palm makes a sweet drink that can be fermented into palm wine. And, of course, there is the fruit. Dates are the nomad's daily bread. Dried and ground, they provide date flour, while their juice makes date honey. Even the date stones are ground and mixed with fodder for cattle or roasted to produce date coffee, a very bitter drink.

deep red dye grow in the oases. The dye is used by North African women to paint designs on their hands and to tint their hair.

The most common animals in Libya are those that are domesticated, including sheep, goats, cattle, horses, camels, and donkeys. Where there is sufficient shade and water, one can also see hyenas, jackals, and wildcats.

In the dry desert areas lies a wilderness empty of life during the day. Most lizards, snakes, and rodents would die in a few minutes in the hot sun; so dune creatures have learned to burrow underground, where it is cooler.

When the sun goes down and the sand cools, animals such as the jerboa come out to feed. With a tail almost as long as its 6-inch (15 cm) body, the

A jerboa

Skinks use their tongues to sniff the air and track prey.

mouse-like jerboa moves in a series of jumps with its forefeet held together, with small carnivores such as fennecs (small foxes) watching for them. Fennecs obtain the water they need by eating jerboas as well as lizards and beetles.

Snakes and lizards are cold-blooded, meaning their blood temperature is not constant. At night their body temperature falls so low that in the morning, they must bask in the sun in order to bring their bodies back to normal working condition. During that time they are vulnerable to predators such as hawks and foxes. If they lie in the sun for too long, they overheat, so they soon dig their way underground for shelter.

The skink is a common desert lizard. It has a wedge-shaped jaw, handy for digging sheltering holes in loose sand, and its eyes are covered with transparent scales. It is sometimes called a sandfish because when it runs, it looks as if it is swimming through the sand.

Skinks are regarded as delicacies by the desert nomads, who gut and roast them on skewers. Skinks are small and easy to take care of, and children in towns sometimes keep them as pets.

Most of the desert gazelle have been hunted for food and skins, but there is one breed of antelope that can be found in small pockets in the Idhan Desert near the Algerian border. This is the lumbering addax antelope, which is highly endangered. It seems to survive without water. Nomads believe that the juice from the vegetable matter in the stomach of an addax can cure any illness, from scorpion bites to food poisoning.

IRRIGATING THE DESERT

In ancient times the Romans built elaborate irrigation systems, as the ruins of huge cisterns indicate. There were apparently abundant supplies of wheat, barley, citrus fruits, olives, and dates.

WHERE THE BUFFALO ROAMED

The central Sahara contains a treasure trove of cave paintings and carved rock art by a hunting people who lived in the area approximately between 12,000 and 4000 BCE. The art shows a much different region than the desert of today—a lush grassland teeming with giant buffalo, elephant herds, and even

hippopotamuses. Scientists believe that a major climate change occurred about five thousand years ago, beginning a process of desertification that gradually turned grassland into barren desert.

Libya's revolutionary leader Colonel Muammar Gaddafi once promised that "the desert will bloom." A three-year plan was launched in 1973, followed by a more ambitious five-year plan in 1976. The aim was to make fuller use of the natural resources, increase agricultural production, and create self-sufficient communities in agricultural areas. Nevertheless, the country still imports 75 percent of its food.

In the coastal areas, small amounts of petroleum waste mixed with other products have been sprinkled on the surface of the sand dunes to prevent wind erosion. This has allowed eucalyptus trees to take root on the dunes. Coarse grass has been planted in square grids to prevent the sand from drifting.

Gaddafi's government constructed a network of dams in the wadis, dry watercourses that become torrents after heavy rains. These dams are used

THE CAMEL

Although motorized transportation is common in Libya, the camel remains valuable for long journeys and is also used for plowing. A camel's speed rarely exceeds 4 miles (6 km) an hour. It can be forced into a rapid trot, but only for a few minutes or it will go lame. Owners look after camels carefully because to own many camels is a sign of great wealth.

Camels can drink 20 gallons (90 liters) of water at one time. But ignore rumors that this water is stored in its hump; the hump is made of fat and does not store water. The camel stores its main supply of liquid in its stomach, which has three sections and can hold over 50 gallons (225 L). When all that is used up, the camel goes on for two or three days on the liquid stored in its body tissues.

The camel is actually an Asiatic animal and was not introduced to the deserts west of the Nile River until the first century BCE. Known as the ship of the desert, the one-humped Arabian camel can survive on dry twigs and can smell water up to a mile away. It lives for forty years or more, and can carry a load of 1,000 pounds (450 kilograms) and travel 25 miles (40 km) a day. Nomadic Libyans make use of every part of a camel carcass. They use its thick hide to make sandals, and get lard from its hump. The people eat the meat of young camels and drink camel's milk, which they use to make cheese. Camel droppings are dried for fuel.

In biblical times, when the Hebrew nation under Gideon fought the various peoples of Canaan, the raiding Midianites that attacked the Israelites rode on camels. The sight of the raiders on these animals—creatures previously considered wild and untamable—frightened the mighty Hebrew soldiers. Even trained camels can be haughty and vicious; they spit, bite, and kick when they are annoyed.

both as water reservoirs and for flood and erosion control. The wadis are heavily settled because soil in their bottoms is often suitable for agriculture, and the high water table in their vicinity makes them logical locations for digging wells. In many wadis, however, the water table is declining at an alarming rate, particularly in areas of intensive agriculture and near urban centers.

FEATHERED FOWL

The birds of Libya include eagles, hawks, vultures, wagtails, owls, ravens, black and white wheatears, partridges, and sandgrouse. The pigeon-like sandgrouse has special water-absorbent feathers that allow it to carry moisture back to its nest to cool its eggs. The noble falcon is seldom seen flying wild, though there are desert sheikhs who keep trained falcons for hunting small game or other birds. The desert lark has a special place in nomadic tradition. Children are warned not to follow it. If they follow the lark a yard or two, and then a few more, they may easily get lost in the desert.

A sandgrouse has a thick layer of down under its feathers to protect it from the extreme heat.

INTERNET LINKS

countrystudies.us/libya/35.htm
This website offers a good overview of Libya's geography.

www.eoearth.org/view/article/168286
This article takes an in-depth look at the Libyan Desert.

geography.howstuffworks.com/africa/geography-of-libya1.htm
This site provides a comprehensive description of the physical geography of Libya.

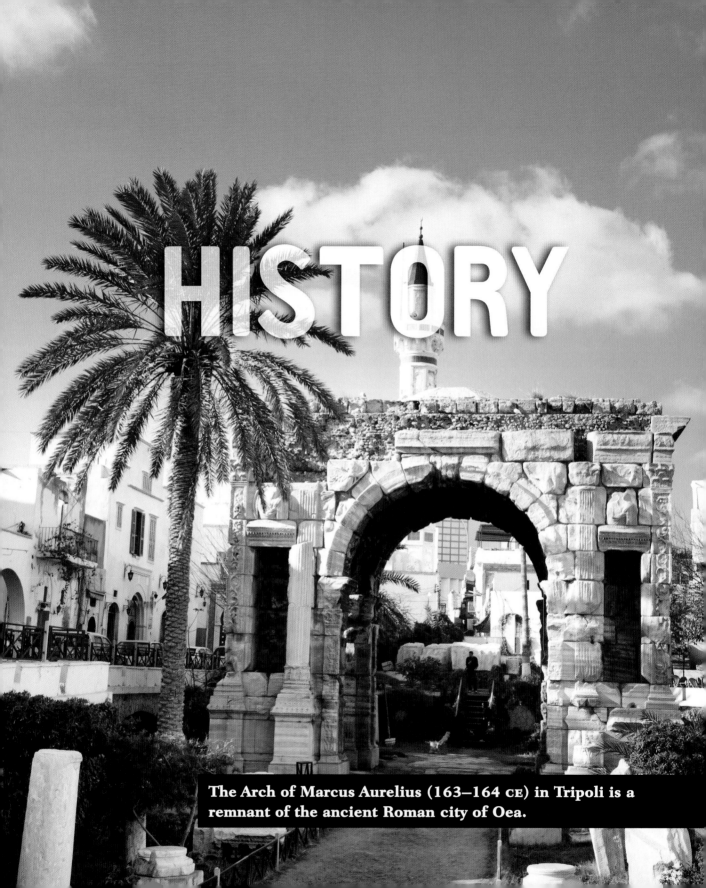

HISTORY

The Arch of Marcus Aurelius (163–164 CE) in Tripoli is a remnant of the ancient Roman city of Oea.

2

For hundreds of years, the name Libya referred to all of Africa except Egypt.

THE LIBYAN REGION HAS BEEN AT the center of armed conflicts almost since the Stone Age. Partly because of its geographical position in the center of North Africa, it has been conquered and reconquered again and again, first by the Phoenicians, then by the Romans, the Arabs, Turks, and Italians. Today, once again, Libya is facing armed chaos with an uncertain outcome.

Around 1000 BCE, Phoenician sailors from what is now Lebanon began to visit the North African coast in search of gold, silver, ivory, apes, and peacocks. They founded the city-state of Carthage (in modern-day Tunisia). Carthage became a great naval and trading center, a rival to Rome. In 146 BCE, after a series of wars known as the Punic Wars, the Romans totally destroyed Carthage and made the region around Carthage part of Rome's growing empire. The Greeks founded the city of Cyrene (in the Al Jabar Al Akhdar region of present-day Libya), one of the cultural centers of the Greco-Roman world. Cyrene was a place of learning, known for its scientists and philosophers. Wine, wool, and medicinal herbs were produced there. In 67 BCE Cyrenaica, together with Crete, became an official province of the Roman Empire.

The Romans built the fine cities of Sabratha, Leptis Magna, and Oea in what is now the Tripolitania part of Libya. After 435 CE, however, Tripolitania fell into the hands of the Vandals and Byzantine Greeks before the area was conquered by the Muslim Arabs in 642 CE.

The United Nations Education, Scientific, and Cultural Organization (UNESCO) has urged all sides involved in the present fighting to preserve Libya's cultural heritage. Libya has five UNESCO World Heritage sites:

Leptis Magna *Leptis Magna was enlarged and embellished by Septimius Severus, Roman emperor from 193 to 211 CE. He was born there and later became emperor. It was one of the most beautiful cities of the Roman Empire, with its imposing public monuments, harbor, marketplace, storehouses, shops, and residential districts. Although Leptis (a Latinized version of its Phoenician name) was comparable to the other Phoenician trading centers of the Syrian coast, like*

Sabratha, after Septimius Severus became emperor in 193 CE, its fortunes improved remarkably. Thanks to him, the renewed Leptis became one of the most beautiful cities of the Roman world. It is still one of the best examples of Severan urban planning. The ancient port, with its artificial basin of some 1.1 million square feet (102,000 square meters), still exists with its quays, jetties, fortifications, storage areas, and temples. The market, an essential element in the everyday life of a large commercial trading center, with its votive arch, colonnades, and shops, has been preserved for the most part.

Cyrene *Cyrene, founded in 630 BCE, was built by Greeks coming from the island of Thera. It was one of the main cities of ancient Greece. Its ruins are located in the valley, in the Jebel Akhdar uplands, in the present-day city of Shahhat in Libya. The ancient city grew to become one of the major cities of ancient Libya, establishing trade relations with other Greek cities of that period. It had its own kings in*

the fifth century BCE, but by 460 BCE it had become a republic. Cyrene was conquered by the Romans around 96 BCE and became a Roman province. Under the Romans, Cyrene remained an important city until it came to an unceremonious end in a massive earthquake that took place in 262 CE.

Sabratha *The archaeological site of Sabratha is in northwestern Libya. Sabratha was established by the Phoenicians around 500 BCE as a trading post for products coming from the African hinterland. It was originally called Sbrt'n. There is a possibility that a village might have already existed in the area when the Phoenicians arrived.*

Old Town of Ghadames *The old town of Ghadames stands in an oasis and is known as "the pearl of the desert." The town is one of the oldest pre-Saharan settlements, and while none of its original buildings remain, it still retains its own architectural style. Houses were organized vertically by function—ground floors were used to store supplies, an upper floor for family, and open-air terraces were reserved for women.*

Rock Art Sites of Tadrart Acacus
Tadrart Acacus is located in a mountainous region, located in the Fezzan, east of the city of Ghat. Thousands of cave paintings in varying styles can be found on cave walls scattered throughout the region. The paintings date from 12,000 BCE to 100 CE and reflect the changes of plant and animal life and also depict the changing ways of life of people who lived in the region.

THE ARRIVAL OF ISLAM

In the seventh century CE, Islamic armies from the Middle East swept westward until they controlled all of North Africa and half of Spain. They brought with them their religion and language. The Arabs were not town dwellers, and the Roman cities were left to the enveloping sand, apart from the central area of Oea, which was maintained as a fort and on which the city of Tripoli now stands.

After the death of the Prophet Muhammad in 632 CE, Muslim rule over the Islamic conquests passed into the hands of the caliphs, the Prophet Muhammad's successors. Libya became part of the area controlled by the legendary Haroun al-Raschid (766—809 CE) who ruled a vast empire from his capital in Baghdad, in what is now Iraq. The empire was called the Abbasid Empire. Al-Rashid appointed a local governor to rule his North African territories from what is now Kairouan in Tunisia.

In 1051, the Arabs in Tunisia, Tripolitania, and Cyrenaica rebelled against the powerful Fatimid caliphs of Cairo, who had taken control of the area from the Abbasids. Not only did the Fatimids send armies to subdue these provinces, but they also sent families and livestock to populate the area. The newcomers intermarried with the local people, and the Arabic language and way of life became a mainstay of Libyan culture.

For more than three hundred years, marauding fleets of pirates based in Tripoli made the North African coast feared by all who sailed the Mediterranean. They seized trading vessels in the Mediterranean, plundered the cargoes, and sold the crews into slavery. In Spain, where the Arab invaders had settled, Christian armies were gathering. In 1510, a European expedition captured Tripoli, and the Order of Knights of the Hospital of Saint John of Jerusalem sent a detachment of soldiers from Malta to build a castle there.

TURKS AND ITALIANS

Troops from the Turkish Ottoman Empire invaded Libya in 1551. They captured Tripoli, encouraged pirate fleets to sail again, and even made expeditions against the Berbers inland. Elite Turkish soldiers, called *janissaries*, settled in

After making the pilgrimage to Mecca, a Berber leader named Sheikh Muhammad ibn Ali al-Sanusi decided that Islam needed strengthening against the persuasive attractions of the Western world. He opened a series of religious lodges. The first was in Mecca, and another in Libya. By 1867 there were fifty lodges in Cyrenaica. The aim of the Sanusi (sahn-OO-see) Muslims was to live pious lives and purify their faith. In due course, this brotherhood of stern-minded Arabs made highly effective warriors against the Italians.

The Sanusi sect became the backbone of Libyan resistance against Italian rule. This was the time of the legendary Sanusi hero Omar al-Mukhtar, a simple country school teacher who led the Libyan resistance. Leading a force of nomadic fighters that rose to six thousand people, Omar led intermittent attacks on Italian communications and supply lines for nearly twenty years. In September 1931, he was wounded and captured in the Green Mountains and subsequently hanged before a crowd of 20,000 Libyans. During World War II, many Sanusis fled to Egypt and joined the Allied forces to continue the fight against the Italians.

Omar al-Mukhtar is arrested by Italian authorities.

Libya and married local women. Libya remained under Turkish influence for three centuries, and buildings from the Turkish period still stand today.

In 1911, Italy declared war on the Ottoman Empire and occupied Libya. Beneath the sand, the Italians found the impressive remains of cities built by their Roman ancestors. They felt they were returning to lands that had once been theirs. (Benito Mussolini was a newspaper editor at that time and strongly criticized the invasion. He was a socialist at that time. He was jailed for opposing the invasion. When he became the dictator of Fascist Italy, he counted Libya and Ethiopia as part of the "new empire.") There was a deliberate attempt by the Italian army to destroy Arab culture. Libyans in the occupied areas were given limited political rights, and those who refused to accept Italian authority were massacred.

Stories are still told of the Italian army's cruelty: how they sealed Bedouin wells, destroyed herds of cattle, and put people into concentration camps. The hanging of Libyans in every city became a daily event. More than 150,000 Italians settled in Libya.

TWO WORLD WARS

World War I caused Italy to loosen its grip on Libya for a brief period, as Italy was occupied with the war in Europe. Many World War II battles were fought across North Africa. The Desert War was a gigantic conflict that swept back and forth through Tunisia, Libya, and Egypt. The Allied armies and the Axis troops advanced and retreated as much as 4,000 miles (6,500 km). Britain's Eighth Army and Germany's Afrika Korps earned their fame as much from battling the Libyan Desert as from battling each other.

An Italian soldier seizes the green Islamic flag during a fight in Tripoli in this illustration from a French newspaper in 1911.

Much of the fighting revolved around the Libyan port of Tobruk. Long lines of gravestones in the desert form the military cemeteries of the Allied and Axis troops. Even today wandering camels and sometimes herdsmen are killed by one of the thousands of landmines that lie buried as deadly souvenirs of the Desert War.

After the war, the victorious Allied powers realized Libya's strategic importance and argued for a long time about who should take over the land. It seemed best to give Libya the chance to make its own choice. So, in 1951, the United Nations declared Libya an independent state, and a national assembly chose Muhammad Idris al-Sanusi as its first monarch.

MONARCHY

King Idris swiftly showed the style of rule he favored—absolute. There was one hotly contested election in 1952, after which Idris banned all political parties, banished most of his relatives to the desert, and deported the leader of the main opposition party. Though improvements were soon made in

Libyan education and health services, the people in power became rich, while the poor remained poor.

As the Western world powers had hoped, Idris welcomed British and US military bases into Libya. Wheelus Air Force Base near Tripoli became a main NATO training base and part of the Western defense system. At the time of independence, Libya was poverty stricken, and its people mostly illiterate. In return for the military bases, the United States and Great Britain provided substantial economic and technical aid.

One of the benefits of having foreign experts in Libya was the discovery of oil fields in the desert. By 1960 there were thirty-five oil wells in production. Exports of petroleum rose from 8.2 million tons (8 million metric tons) in 1962 to over 77 million tons (70 million t) in 1966. Much of the profit went to the foreign countries that had done the drilling. Unfortunately, little of Libya's newfound wealth was passed to the Libyan people. Many Libyans wished for a new government. Some had been planning for many years to organize a coup.

King Idris in 1951

THE REVOLUTION

In the early morning of September 1, 1969, while King Idris was on vacation in Turkey, Libyan army officers captured the state palace in Tripoli in a bloodless coup. A few hours later, the leader of the coup, Muammar Abu Minyar al-Gaddafi, seized a radio station in Benghazi and broadcast the news. He told listening Libyans that the monarchy had been replaced by a republic. Many Libyan army units had wanted to seize control for months, but Gaddafi's group acted first.

The king expected the United States or Great Britain to restore him to the throne, but neither nation wished to stir up trouble in the Middle East. Idris soon announced that he was passing the throne on to his son, Crown Prince Hassan al-Reda. The prince was promptly arrested and hastily agreed to urge Libyans to support the new regime. Idris went into exile in Egypt, where he died in 1983.

In an interview with an Egyptian editor, Gaddafi expressed the hope that Egypt's president, Gamal Abdel Nasser, whom Gaddafi admired greatly, would take over the country. When that did not happen, Gaddafi promoted himself as colonel and was automatically accepted as chairman of the new government. At the age of twenty-seven, he became the ruler of Libya. His main aims quickly became apparent: to build unity among the Arab countries, to create a Libyan socialist republic based on Islamic law, and to destroy Israel, which he regarded as the prime enemy of the Arab world.

THE LONE FALCON

Gaddafi was born to a family of desert nomads. As one of his grandfathers had been killed by the Italian invaders, and his father and uncle imprisoned for resisting them, young Gaddafi learned to hate Europeans at an early age.

By the age of ten, his teachers recognized that he was remarkably intelligent. He rose to the top of his class and was promoted swiftly. One of his early fascinations was the radio. He would listen to it for hours, often going without food so that he could buy new batteries. The Voice of the Arabs programs broadcast from Egypt allowed Gaddafi to listen to President Nasser, who became his hero.

While attending high school in Sabha, Gaddafi began to recruit secret cells of students with the plan to overthrow the Libyan monarchy. The plan leaked and Gaddafi was expelled. Undaunted, he attended another school, graduated with honors, and entered the University of Libya. He continued planning to overthrow the king. After earning a degree in law, he joined the army and steadily recruited more followers. By August 1969 Gaddafi was the acting adjutant of the Libyan Signal Corps. With most of Libya's seven thousand-strong army already sympathetic to the revolutionary cause, he launched the coup on September 1, 1969. Four months after the coup, Gaddafi married a teacher at a midnight ceremony attended by Nasser. The marriage failed and they divorced after the birth of one son. In July 1970 Gaddafi married a nurse, who bore him more children.

Gaddafi created controversy in the Middle East and beyond. After Nasser died in 1970, his successor, Anwar Sadat, did not share Gaddafi's dream for Arab unity. This led to the deterioration of relations with Egypt. When Sadat tried to make peace with Israel, Gaddafi rallied several Arab states to freeze relations with Egypt. On the international stage, he astounded politicians and rulers with his lack of tact. On the domestic front, Italians in Libya were expelled in 1970, and an American airbase, the Wheelus base, was vacated in June 1970 and returned to Libyan control.

Obsessed with power and the desire for perfection in his country, Gaddafi instituted the death penalty for anyone who dared to engage in political activity against him.

Colonel Muammar Gaddafi speaks to the people in Tripoli after the coup in 1969.

Strikes were forbidden. The Arab Socialist Union became Libya's only political party. To support his ideals, Gaddafi produced the *Green Book* in three volumes, setting out his theories for the perfect democracy, the perfect economy, and the way of life that he called the Third Universal Way. He had three unshakable obsessions: revolution, Islam, and Arab unity.

In an effort to show that he was still a humble Arab at heart, Gaddafi declared his only title as "Brother Colonel." He was photographed in his family tent wearing Arab robes, although his usual dress was an army uniform. He roamed the streets in disguise, sharing the talk of the Libyan people. Slightly built with a deep, quiet voice and boyish grin, he walked with bent shoulders and hands in his pockets.

CULTURAL REVOLUTION

On April 15, 1973, the day on which the Prophet Muhammad's birthday was being celebrated, the announcement of Libya's new Cultural Revolution was made. It was designed to uphold the ideals of the Al-Fatah revolution (in 1969, when Gaddafi came to power) and give the country to its people. It was also a further excuse to purge the country of any dissident elements. Many citizens thought that to expel communists and capitalists was one thing;

to imprison thousands of peaceful Libyans who happened to disagree was something altogether different.

Arabic was made the official language by a Revolutionary Committee firmly guided by Gaddafi. Anything printed in English or Italian was removed. Following strict Islamic law, alcohol, revealing clothes, bars, casinos, and unsuitable literature were banned. Hundreds of books were burned.

Nevertheless, the ordinary person in Libya found that the general quality of life began to improve. Roads, hospitals, and schools were built. Irrigation projects were planned to increase food production. The factories and assets of foreign companies were nationalized by the state. By 1977, Libya was the richest country on the African continent.

INTERNATIONAL TERRORISM

Certain that Libya had taken the right step toward freedom, Gaddafi began to support other revolutionary movements around the world. In the 1970s and 1980s Libyan wealth backed rebel terrorists in Northern Ireland, the Palestine Liberation Organization, the Basque separatist movement in Spain, and South African black activists fighting apartheid. In 1979, Gaddafi sent troops to support the brutal dictator Idi Amin in Uganda. It is suspected that there may have been as many as twenty camps in Libya training more than seven thousand terrorists for subversive activities around the world.

In March 1986 US warships deliberately sailed into the Gulf of Sirte, which Gaddafi had claimed as Libyan waters. Libya instantly launched an attack that backfired—Libyan vessels were sunk or damaged. Days later a series of terrorist attacks around the world seemed to implicate Libya. On April 15, 1986, US President Ronald Reagan ordered major bombing raids against Tripoli and Benghazi, dubbed Operation El Dorado Canyon, aimed at Gaddafi's support of terrorism. The raids killed forty-five Libyan military and government personnel as well as fifteen civilians.

In 1988, Gaddafi was believed to have been involved in the bombing of a commercial airplane in the skies over Lockerbie, Scotland, in which hundreds of people were killed. When Gaddafi refused to hand over the two Libyans suspected in the bombing, many countries severed diplomatic ties with Libya.

In 1992, the United Nations imposed sanctions on Libya for its continued harboring of the two suspects. In 1999, Gaddafi finally agreed to let the men stand trial in the Netherlands under Scottish law, and the UN sanctions were suspended. The trial came to an end in 2001, with one suspect jailed and the other set free. In August 2003, Libya admitted responsibility for the Lockerbie incident and the United Nations agreed to lift sanctions. However, the United States continued to boycott relations with Libya.

Libyans tend to the injured after the US raid on Tripoli in 1986.

THE LIBYAN CIVIL WAR

The impetus of the Libyan civil war began on February 15, 2011, as a series of peaceful protests that were met with military force by the Gaddafi regime. The protests escalated into an uprising that spread across the country. Forces opposed to Gaddafi established a government based in Benghazi named the National Transitional Council. Its goal was the overthrow of the Gaddafi-led government, followed by democratic elections.

The United Nations Security Council passed an initial resolution freezing the assets of Gaddafi and ten members of his inner circle, and restricting their travel. The resolution also referred the actions of the government to the International Criminal Court for investigation. An arrest warrant for Gaddafi was issued on June 27. In early March, Gaddafi's forces rallied, pushed eastward, and reclaimed several coastal cities before attacking Benghazi. A further UN resolution authorized member states to establish and enforce a no-fly zone over Libya.

The capital city of Tripoli fell to the rebels on August 23, 2011. Gaddafi and his family fled the capital and were eventually captured when his convoy traveling to Sirte was caught in a NATO airstrike. Gaddafi took refuge in a large drainage pipe but was found, captured, and then shot to death on October 20. Libyans all around the world rejoiced at the death of the mercurial leader

The acronym ISIS stands for the "Islamic State of Iraq and Syria." It is also called ISIL, the "Islamic State of Iraq and the Levant" or just IS for "Islamic State." Yet another name for this militant group is "Daesh." Whatever it's called, ISIS has thrown a chill upon the entire Middle East.

Made up largely of extremist Sunni Arabs from Iraq and Syria, the organization is dedicated to violent jihad, *or struggle against the enemies of Islam. As of September 2015, the militant group had conquered a territory occupied by ten million people in Iraq and Syria and was gaining territory in Libya. ISIS calls itself a state, or nation, as well as a caliphate. A caliphate is a form of Islamic government led by a caliph—a person considered a political and religious successor to the Prophet Muhammad, and a leader of the entire Muslim community.*

The collapse of the Ottoman Empire a hundred years ago marked the end of the last caliphate. ISIS means for the new caliphate to be the successor to the caliphates that once ruled the entire Islamic world.

ISIS's goals are to unite all Muslims under one caliphate and to reconquer all lands that Muslims once ruled. Its tactics are brutal. ISIS has shocked the world with its mass executions

Activists in India burn the black flag of ISIS in 2015. They want their government to stop the militant group from entering their country.

of Christians and Westerners. It has been designated as a terrorist organization by the United Nations, the European Union, the United Kingdom, the United States, India, Indonesia, Turkey, Saudi Arabia, and other governments. More than sixty countries are at war with ISIS, yet its territory keeps expanding. To many people, the black flag of ISIS spreads fear in the desert much as, in times past, the black skull and crossbones of pirate flags once spread fear on the sea.

who had ruled over their oil-rich country for forty-two years. When the civil war ended, US President Barack Obama pledged to work with the new Libyan government as a partner and said the United States was "committed to the Libyan people."

US relations with the new Libyan government were thrust into the spotlight on September 11, 2012. Gunmen attacked and firebombed the US liaison office in Benghazi, killing four Americans, including Ambassador J. Christopher Stevens. Those responsible have never been caught and brought to justice. On May 27, the US advised all US citizens in the country to leave immediately and avoid any travel due to the dangerous and chaotic situation in the country.

Since then, Libya has dissolved in armed chaos marked by the ominous rise of ISIS, the terrorist army that has already taken over much of Iraq and Syria and thrown the entire Middle East into bloody turmoil.

INTERNET LINKS

www.bbc.com/news/world-africa-13755445
This site from the BBC provides a clear history time line for Libya from prehistory to the present.

www.nytimes.com/projects/2013/benghazi/#/?chapt=0
"A Deadly Mix in Benghazi" is a revealing look at the 2012 attacks against the US diplomatic mission and CIA compound in Benghazi, Libya.

www.telegraph.co.uk/culture/culturepicturegalleries/9909936/Roman-ruins-in-Libya-aerial-photographs-by-Jason-Hawkes.html?frame=2500368
This website has some amazing aerial photographs of the ruins of Roman Libya that show the durability of Roman construction.

GOVERNMENT

Libyans in Tripoli hang flags to celebrate their liberation from the Gaddafi regime on November 5, 2011.

3

I N MODERN TIMES, LIBYA HAS GONE through a number of governments, from the dictatorship of King Idris, to the dictatorship of Muammar Gaddafi, to the present situation of two rival national governments.

Forces from the Libya Dawn militia fire at Operation Dignity forces loyal to Libya's internationally recognized government in April 2015.

In June 2014, Salwa Bughaighis, an outspoken human rights lawyer and rebel activist against Gaddafi, was shot dead in her home on the day the Libyan people were voting to select a new parliament. Her assassination signaled a turning point from bad to worse in the Libyan uprisings, and the dashing of hopes for a democratic, modern Libya.

"Racism, barbarism, and savagery are deep-rooted in the ethics of the Western imperialist colonialists . . . They are determined that African unity will not be established."

"All the efforts [of the Organization of African Unity] should be directed to the liberation of Palestine and South Africa, and the destruction of the racist regimes."

"We have given training to thousands of Africans—on Libyan soil—who took part in the liberation of a number of African countries."

In July 2015, a court in Tripoli sentenced Seif al-Islam al-Gaddafi, the son of the former dictator Muammar Gaddafi, along with eight other Gaddafi government officials, to death. They were convicted of war crimes against the Libya people during the 2011 uprising against Gaddafi.

The constitution approved by the United Nations in 1951 set up an elected house of representatives with fifty-five members and an upper house or senate, half of whom were nominated by the king. The king also had the power to appoint his own provincial governors, to veto legislation, and to dissolve the lower house completely if he so wished.

Within two years all political parties were banned. Idris made no attempt to meet the desires of his people by changing Libya from a monarchy (rule by a king or queen) to a republic (rule by an elected president).

The king's unpopularity became the grounds for revolution. The coup in September 1969 left Idris in exile and put Gaddafi in power. A twelve-man revolutionary council was appointed, with Gaddafi as chairman. Libya was proclaimed "an Arab democratic and free republic." Ethnic leaders soon lost much of their power, and traditional interior boundaries ceased to exist. There was then only one political party: the Arab Socialist Union, formed in 1971, which allowed all Libyans to participate in the government through local popular congresses.

In March 1977, the General People's Congress renamed the country the Socialist People's Libyan Arab Jamahiriya. (*Jamahiriya* is a word invented by Gaddafi, meaning "a state of the masses.") With all power delegated to various committees, Libya claimed to be the first and only country in the world with "no government." People learned to talk of "the authorities" rather than "the government."

THE GREAT *GREEN BOOK*

Between 1976 and 1979 Gaddafi produced his three-volume *Green Book*, outlining his "final solution to the problem of governing" in three points: The solution to the problems of democracy is to give authority to the people. Democracy is not government; it is the formation of committees everywhere, and "supervision of the people by the people." The solution to economic problems is socialism. People should be "partners, not wage workers." They should control the places where they work and own homes. The solution to social problems is the Third Universal Theory. This emphasizes the importance of family and tribal unity, the role of women (slightly inferior to men, and primarily made for marriage and bearing children), the protection of minorities, and "how the blacks will prevail in the world."

According to Gaddafi, these theories were intended to steer Libya away from the evils of Western-style democracy with its free-market capitalism and also Marxist communism with its all-powerful politburo.

Khalifa Al-Ghweil, the acting prime minister of the self-declared government in Tripoli, delivers a speech in August 2015.

THE TWO RIVAL GOVERNMENTS

On the national level, Libya's two competing governments are engaged in a massive power struggle. One is the Tripoli-based General National Congress (New GNC). This body, formed by politicians from the parties that lost the June 2014 elections in Libya, is supported by Islamist revolutionary groups operating under the banner of Libyan Dawn. This faction captured the Libyan capital of Tripoli after a five-week battle. It has set up its own government, with a former Islamic fighter, Omar al-Hasi, as its declared prime minister. It is strongly backed by the Muslim Brotherhood, a powerful organization that supports government based on the Qur'an, Islam's holy book, rather than Western forms of government.

Libya's other would-be national government is the Council of Deputies, democratically elected in 2014 and headquartered in Tobruk. The Tobruk

The Muslim Brotherhood was founded in Cairo, Egypt, in 1928 by Hassan al-Banna. Al-Banna called for a return to an original Islam because he felt that modern Islam had been corrupted by Western influences. By 1936, the Brotherhood had eight hundred members. Only two years later, in 1938, it had 200,000 members and by 1948, it had an estimated half million members. Today, it has millions of members in Egypt, Libya, and in other Muslim countries.

In 1948, a student member of the Brotherhood assassinated Egypt's Prime Minister Mahmud Nokrashi. Soon afterwards, men believed to be linked to the government killed the Brotherhood's founder, Hassan al-Banna. In 1954, the Egyptians banned the Muslim Brotherhood as a political party. Despite this, the Brotherhood grew throughout the 1980s as a part of a general growth in interest in Islam, and the US-led invasion of Iraq in 2003 prompted a spike in membership.

The Brotherhood claims it has been persecuted and has seen its members arrested and tortured. Today, it engages in charity work with the poor, supplying food and clothing to the needy, setting up hospitals, and teaching the illiterate.

government has been internationally recognized as the official Libyan government under the leadership of Prime Minister Abdullah al-Thinni and has the loyalty of the Libyan Army. The military alliance supporting this government uses the banner "Operation Dignity." It favors a less Islamic radical government when compared to the GNC. Both rival governments claim to be the true representatives of the Libyan people. On January 16, 2015, the opposing factions supporting these two governments agreed on a ceasefire, but the country remains in chaos as other groups, including ISIS and Boku Haram, roam the countryside.

Abdullah al-Thinni, prime minister of Libya's Tobruk-based government, speaks to the media in March 2015.

INTERNET LINKS

www.aljazeera.com/news/2015/04/libya-tale-governments-150404075631141.html

"Libya: A Tale of Two Governments" is a good article explaining the opposing factions behind the two governments.

www.bbc.com/news/world-africa-27492354

This is a 2014 profile of the ex-Gaddafi general who is a force on the Libyan political scene.

www.theguardian.com/world/2014/aug/31/tripoli-residents-libya-dawn-islamist-militias

The Guardian newspaper reports on Libya Dawn.

ECONOMY

An Egyptian worker harvests dates from a date palm tree in Tajura, Libya, a coastal town not far from Tripoli.

4

FOR MUCH OF ITS HISTORY, LIBYA'S economy was based on the limited farming along its Mediterranean coast. Much of the rest of the country was considered desert wasteland and economically useless.

The 1959 discovery of oil changed Libya's fortunes. The increase in the price of oil in the 1970s made Libya the richest country in Africa. The oil industry provided employment and a high income for many Libyans. However, the US trade embargo with Libya, which began in 1982, and the UN sanctions in 1992 had a devastating effect on the economy. The standard of living declined rapidly and basic materials and food became scarce. Gaddafi's attempts to make Libya self-sufficient met with little success and although a few countries continued to trade with Libya, there was widespread discontent. When the United Nations suspended sanctions in 1999, life for Libyans improved as the economy began to recover. War and the rapid drop in the price of oil have devastated the Libyan oil industry.

PETROLEUM

Libya's deserts conceal the largest underground reserves of oil in Africa and the eighth largest in the world. The reserves amount to about 30 billion barrels of oil. Libyan crude oil is particularly popular because it has little sulfur; it causes less pollution and is less expensive to process into petroleum. The nickname for such oil is "sweet crude."

The Sirte basin is responsible for most of Libya's oil output. It contains about 80 percent of the country's proven oil reserves, which amount to 44 billion barrels, the largest in Africa.

In the 1960s, when these reserves were first tapped, Libya was the greatest oil producer in Africa. By 1965 Libya was the sixth-largest exporter in the world, and in 1969, its oil output exceeded even that of Saudi Arabia. Libya's oil production was severely restricted as a result of UN trade sanctions, but since the sanctions were suspended in 1999, many European and Arab countries have resumed drilling and refining operations in the country. The countries include Saudi Arabia, South Korea, Germany, Italy, Spain, and Canada.

Gaddafi invested heavily in Libya's oil refineries and pipelines. Oil and petroleum products made up more than 97 percent of exports and account for a large number of jobs in industry and construction. Libya had three refineries capable of handling about 340,000 barrels a day. Pipelines up to 180 miles (290 km) long stretch from the oil fields, mostly in the desert off the Gulf of Sirte, to tanker terminals on the coast.

During the Iran—Iraq War in the 1980s, oil prices skyrocketed, only to collapse in 1986. Although by that time all Libyan oil had been nationalized

A Libyan oil worker passes by a refinery inside the Brega oil complex in Libya.

so no foreign company could make a profit, the drop in price badly affected Libya's economy. Fresh reserves of offshore oil and natural gas were found near Benghazi in the 1990s. They contributed further to Libya's oil wealth. It is possible that the present oil reserves in Libya could run out within the next fifty years. When the antigovernment protests erupted, Libya was the twelfth-largest oil exporter in the world.

Libya, an OPEC (Organization of Petroleum Exporting Countries, an intergovernmental group made up of twelve countries) member, was Africa's fourth-largest oil producer after Nigeria, Algeria, and Angola—it produced up to 1.8 million barrels per day. Eighty percent of its "sweet crude" exports were sold to European countries, particularly Italy. Since the start of the civil war, oil production was cut by half. During the war, the price per barrel shot up to a two-and-a-half-year high amid investor fears of a drop in production. Libya's "sweet crude" oil cannot be easily replaced in the production of gasoline, diesel, and jet fuel, particularly by the many European and Asian refineries that are not equipped to refine "sour" crude, which is higher in sulfur content.

Many of essential pipelines were heavily damaged during the conflict and oil exports came virtually to halt. It is expected that repairs to the sector's infrastructure will cost hundreds of millions of dollars. Exports only resumed in September 2011. Oil production in Libya in May 2015 averaged 430,000 barrels per day, down from 1.5 million in 2013.

INDUSTRY

Libya boasts iron and steel complexes, an aluminum plant, and chemical complexes for natural salts. The most important industries in the public sector are processed foods (popular local products include canned tomato paste and tuna), soft drinks, tobacco, clothing, footwear, leather, wood, chemicals, and metal goods. Although in the past many factories were small and did not employ more than a hundred people, with heavy investment in large-scale complexes, industry now supports 23 percent of the workforce. Esparto grass is a commercial crop, and a state-controlled factory processes it for export. There are also factories making rugs and cloth from imported materials.

The emphasis on petroleum and industry has resulted in an increase in the number of Libyans living near Tripoli and Benghazi. Both these cities are surrounded by slums as well as military installations. The population drift to the towns has caused serious problems. As in other countries, urban migration has led to housing shortages, and health and lifestyle have suffered. As there are not enough skilled laborers, Libya requires many foreign workers, who often demand the best salaries and houses.

Since Libya's rebel uprising began in February 2011, the country's industrial production has ground to a halt. Libyans now rely extensively on neighboring Tunisia and Egypt for their food imports. The industrial city of Sfax in Tunisia is getting a boost from its neighbor, Libya. However, the Libyan revolution has had a twofold impact on Tunisia. Many Tunisian businesses have been forced to close their operations in Libya. Critical remittances have dried up as thousands of Tunisian workers headed home. And this small North African country is overwhelmed by thousands of refugees who fled Libya.

AGRICULTURE

Although agriculture is practiced by 18 percent of the workforce, Libya depends on imports in most foods. Climatic conditions and poor soils limit farm output, and domestic food production meets about 25 percent of demand. However, things changed after the discovery of oil. The petroleum business produced get-rich-quick dreams among Libyans. There has been a growing flood of migrants from the farms to the towns. In 1960 about 70 percent of the population worked on the land; today the figure stands at less than 17 percent. Even the commercial farmers live in city houses and travel out each day to their farms on the Al-Jifarah Plain.

Less than 2 percent of the land is arable, and less than 4 percent is suitable for raising livestock. Farming produces only 7 percent of Libya's gross domestic product, and the yield per acre is the lowest of all North African countries. Nevertheless, improved irrigation has brought more areas under cultivation, and farmers are encouraged to use cooperative methods.

The main crops are wheat, olives, barley, dates, peanuts, and citrus fruits. All are grown near the coast except dates and figs, which are grown in the oases. There are serious shortages of flour, rice, and non-citrus fruits. Although Libya has nearly 1,118.5 miles (1,800 km) of coastline and the second-largest continental shelf in the Mediterranean, its waters are not particularly rich in plankton needed to sustain fishing waters. In fact, Libya has had to import most of its food due to the underdevelopment of agriculture. The civil war has not been kind to the agricultural sector, with most activities grinding to a halt.

SOUK TO SUPERMARKET

Visitors shopping in the markets, or *souks*, of Tripoli will notice the absence of valuable articles such as handcrafted metalwork, quality leather goods, and Persian carpets. The gold jewelry for which Tripoli became famous is no more. Shoppers can look in vain for the old-style market stalls, called souks, such as the Souk of the Perfumers or the Souk of the Saddlers and Leatherworkers.

In 1981, Gaddafi tried to close all privately owned shops. He considered merchants "parasites" who produced nothing themselves but made money from the masses. So he encouraged the workers to seize control. They did. Most businesses with more than five employees were controlled by a workers' committee. Gaddafi wanted people to shop only at state-registered supermarkets.

A Libyan worker guides the fruit in an olive oil factory.

The system failed badly. Poor organization and interference by state committees caused bottlenecks in supply. Basic goods became unobtainable. Shopping was done on the black market. Gigantic state factories continued to create expensive goods nobody wanted to buy. In 1983, more than two-thirds of the country's food had to be imported. By 1985 Gaddafi was urging Libyans to eat camel meat to reduce the amount of beef and mutton being imported. It is hardly surprising that one of Libya's present aims is to be self-sufficient in food production.

Eventually the lack of small businesses was recognized as a problem, and in 1988, the private sector (mostly partnerships offering employment to a community) was reestablished. Many businesses reopened and food products were easier to find, but it was not enough to ensure a steady supply of goods to the cities. More than two decades later, Libya still imports 75 percent of its food.

TRANSPORTATION

Overall, 29,571 miles (47,590 km) of Libya's 51,698 miles (83,200 km) of road are paved. Most Libyans travel by bus. Cars are very expensive because they are all imported. US-made vehicles are banned. Libya had a functioning railroad until 1965, when it was dismantled. In the 1990s, the Libyan government began to build two railroad lines: one that would run from the Tunisian border to Tripoli and Mistratah, then stretch south to the desert town of Sabha, where iron ore is mined, and the other slated to link the Egyptian border to the coastal town of Tobruk. Although they were planned for completion in 1994, both lines are not yet finished, although an Egyptian and a Spanish company have been hired to supply parts. All construction on these railroads has ceased as a result of the war.

MODERN LIVING

For years Libyan government posters have proclaimed "a house for all" or "a car for all." This dream is fast approaching reality for many urbanites, although the house may be no more than an apartment in a hastily constructed building.

However, many Libyans now think there is little point in working toward personal wealth when there is no stability in the country. The society that was created by Gaddafi's high ideals is riddled with incompetence, corruption, and apathy. Few officials on the hundreds of committees are willing to take responsibility for decisions, as many have been arrested for "failing" the new society. Part of the reason for the uprising was disillusionment with the Gaddafi government and leadership.

In May 1980 a new currency was introduced. Anyone possessing more than $2,100 worth of the old currency received no more than a receipt for

The Great Man-Made River is a network of pipes that supplies water to the coastal cities and towns in Libya from the Nubian Sandstone Aquifer System fossil aquifer. It is the world's largest irrigation project.

It is the largest underground network of pipes (1,752 miles/2,820 km) and aqueducts in the world. It consists of more than 1,300 wells, most of these more than 1,640 feet (500 m) deep, and supplies 239 million cubic feet (6.5 million cubic meters) of fresh water per day to the cities of Tripoli, Benghazi, Sirte, and elsewhere. Gaddafi described it as the "Eighth Wonder of the World."

Although the Great Man-Made River is impressive, experts think that the water table in the areas from which the water is being pumped may drop, threatening the supply to local oases. There is little hope of these deep water reserves being replenished if depleted. The thick, sandy dunes of the Sahara have so far protected underground water supplies from evaporation, but there is not sufficient rainfall to replenish them if they disappear. Within a century they could run dry.

Some of Libya's bank notes still bear the image of Gaddafi.

the excess. All wealth was collected by the state, to be redistributed when necessary. Many Libyans were found to have been hiding money in their houses.

Since the UN sanctions were suspended in 1999, numerous foreign development projects have improved the quality of life in the country. Most Libyans have access to proper sewage, water, electricity, and telephone services. Water remains scarce, and a purification plant has been opened in Tobruk. Construction has begun on a huge desalination plant near Tripoli to purify seawater. However, in view of the escalating debts owed to foreign contractors, it seems unlikely that anything other than essential projects will be completed.

MIGRANT WORKERS

An estimated 32 percent of Libyan citizens were unemployed in 2014, and about one-third live below the national poverty line. In 2011, when Gaddafi was overthrown, more than 16 percent of families had none of their members earning a stable income, while 43.3 percent of the families in Libya had just one member earning a stable income. Despite one of the highest unemployment rates in the region, there was a consistent labor shortage, with more than a million migrant workers present on the market. These migrant workers formed the bulk of the refugees leaving Libya after the beginning of hostilities.

THE NEW ECONOMY

With the bloody and dark days of the civil war behind them, it was hoped that Libya's economy would be able to grow and develop. Under Gaddafi, the country's economy was dominated by oil, which generated about 80 percent of Gaddafi's regime's revenue. However, little of the revenue generated trickled down to ordinary Libyans. Gaddafi's iron grip on the industry, as well a corrupt government, stifled the growth of other sectors.

In response to the civil war, the UN Security Council and other governments such as the United States and Britain froze an estimated $150 billion of Libyan assets. With the death of Gaddafi, the UN, United States, Britain, and other counties lifted sanctions on the Libyan central bank, freeing up much needed finances. The cashflow was to go toward paying salaries as well as restoring key services in the country, but the continuing chaos in the country has all but destroyed the effort.

"The agricultural revolution will enable the Libyan people to earn their living, to eat freely the food that was normally imported from overseas—this is freedom, this is independence, and this is the revolution."

—Muammar Gaddafi, on the Great Man-Made River Project

INTERNET LINKS

www.coldwarstudies.com/2011/03/24/cold-war-libyaall-about-oil
This site explores how the discovery of oil in Libya affected the Cold War and the worldwide struggle between the United States and the Soviet Union.

country.eiu.com/libya
This site provides a concise summary of Libya's economy in 2015.

ENVIRONMENT

A herd of camels drinks at a traditional watering hole in the Libyan Desert.

5

PERHAPS MORE THAN MOST countries, Libya is a prisoner of its natural environment—a narrow strip of fertile land along the Mediterranean coast and a vast hinterland of barren desert. This environment has shaped Libya's history, economy, and the customs of its people.

Lake Gaberoun is one of the largest and most beautiful lakes in the Ubari Sand Sea of the Libyan Desert.

A man draws water in the middle of a vast expanse of sand dunes in Libya.

Libya, of course, is mostly desert, a difficulty for a nation that wants to produce enough food to feed its people. It has been the dream of Libyan leaders since ancient times to create a self-sufficient Libya in terms of agricultural production, and industry and trade as well.

When Gaddafi came to power in 1969, the country underwent intensive industrialization—when the government could pay for it. Projects such as the Great Man-Made River transformed the topography of the North African country but with serious consequences for the natural environment.

Some of the most arid areas of the Sahara Desert are found in Libya, where no animals or vegetation can survive. Droughts occur frequently and sometimes last as long as two years. It is no surprise that the country's main environmental issues revolve around water: its sources, its distribution, and its purity. Traditionally, Bedouin herders relied on regional wells and oases, but population pressures now place so much strain on the desert ecosystem that alternative sources of water must be found.

Libya's drive toward development does not always take into account the environmental consequences of rapid industrialization. Although the country has signed many international agreements, including those on desertification, climate change, marine dumping, and hazardous waste, progress does not always take into account the long-term effects of the new projects. Many generations later, Libyans may find that what initially brought them prosperity has, in fact, made things worse.

WATER

In a desert country brimming with oil wells and petroleum resources, water is a scarce commodity. On the coast, desalination plants remove dissolved minerals (mostly salt and other sediments) from Mediterranean seawater, but the process is expensive. It costs several dollars to produce 35.3 cubic feet (1 cubic m) of desalinated water. In addition desalination plants are extremely inefficient and extract only 15 to 50 percent fresh water from seawater.

In the 1960s, a team searching for oil fields deep underground discovered a vast sea of aquifers under Libya's southern desert. Aquifers are great pools of fresh water trapped beneath layers of rock. Libya's southern aquifers were formed many thousands of years ago, when the Mediterranean Sea reached all the way to the Tibesti Mountains near Libya's border with Chad. Geological activity created the ranges of the Green Mountains, and basins were formed under the rocks beneath them. From 38,000 to 10,000 years ago, Libya had ample rainfall, and over the millennia, water gradually seeped through sedimentary rock to collect in the underground pools. The aquifers, undisturbed for ages, are now being drained to provide fresh water for Libya's cities and farms. About three-quarters of the Libyan population depend on water that is piped in from the Nubian Sandstone Aquifer System. The pipe through which most of the water is channeled is known as the Great Man-Made River.

Men enjoy the cascading waters released from a reservoir at a celebration for the Man-Made River project.

THE PRESSURES OF AGRICULTURE

With water so scarce, it is surprising that Libya can produce even a quarter of its food needs. In recent decades, many local aquifers have dried up and filled with salt water from the sea. Water tainted with salt and high in minerals kills crops and contaminates the entire aquifer.

Under the North African sun, evaporation rates are high. Half of all water used for irrigation is lost under the sun's burning rays. Traditional farming methods are inefficient, and much water is wasted during transportation or

Most people mistakenly think that the desert consists only of sand and rocks. The Sahara Desert, of which Libya is a part, has varied ecosystems of plant, animal, and insect life. Small plants germinate quickly after the rains, and fields of colorful flowers carpet the desert for days or weeks afterward. The plants must grow and reproduce quickly under the desert sun to escape dehydration and death. Still, seeds can lie buried under the Saharan sands for up to a decade until there is enough rain for growth, when once again the desert blooms.

Although the Libyan Desert is one of the hottest and driest areas of the Sahara, reptiles and insects have adapted well to the challenges of survival. Lizards and desert snakes burrow under the ground during the day to escape the hot desert sun but come out to bask in the gentle warmth of morning and evening. Scorpions burrow deep into the sand and impart a dangerous and sometimes lethal sting to anyone who unwittingly steps in their path. Around the desert oases there are mosquitoes, which breed in any stagnant water they can find and plague the population, even in one of the driest and most remote areas of the world.

Because of increased development and population pressure, the mammals of Libya face increased danger and many species are in decline. The famous Barbary lion of North Africa, used in bloody games at the Coliseum during the days of the Roman Empire, is now found only in special breeding areas. In the early twentieth century it was hunted almost to extinction. Now there are none left in the wild. City people increasingly hunt the ibex (right), a small gazelle perfectly adapted to rocky and dry terrain, and they are quickly becoming an endangered species. Unfortunately, Libyans are not aware of the pressures they are placing on their

environment or the plight of endangered animals that live within their borders. Many international organizations, such as the African Conservation Foundation and the World Wildlife Fund, are starting programs to save the desert species.

watering. To keep their land productive, Libyan farmers use 1,627 tons (1,476 t) of fertilizer per square mile (570,000 kilograms per sq km) of land—the twenty-third-highest use of fertilizer in the world. In 2003, Libya signed an agreement with the UN Food and Agricultural Organization (FAO) for more than $21 million of agricultural aid, which would modernize and improve seed production in the country.

Food accounts for 20 percent of Libya's imports. This creates dependence on the outside world. Libya hopes to not only become self-sufficient but also to return to being the breadbasket of North Africa, a position it held in antiquity. That might not be realistic because climatic changes over the last four thousand years have resulted in a steady increase in deserts.

A huge sprinkler system irrigates Libyan agricultural fields.

THE EXPANDING DESERT

Ten thousand years ago, the deserts of Libya were green and lush with rolling plains and abundant wildlife. What is now the Sahara Desert even sported tropical rain forest high in the mountains. Scientists believe that eight thousand years ago, the Earth tilted slightly on its axis, with devastating results. The plains that had been fertile dried up and the desert rapidly claimed what had once been productive farmland. To this day the process continues and desertification is a serious problem in Libya. Already 95 percent of the country is desert, and agricultural land is of poor quality.

The deserts and their borders are very fragile ecosystems. Any change in rainfall has a dramatic effect on vegetation. Desertification occurs when the area that borders a desert, called a transition zone, comes under pressure from increasing human population. Herds of livestock trample the plant life and harden the soil so it is more vulnerable to wind and rain erosion. Overgrazing destroys what is left. Firewood collection eventually destroys the trees. The deserts of Libya thus look destined for expansion.

THE FRAGILE SEA

Since the days of the early Phoenician settlers, life in Libya has revolved around the Mediterranean coast. Most oceans and seas filter waste and debris efficiently, although man-made pollutants, such as plastics and metals, are becoming an increasing problem.

The Mediterranean Sea is one of the most polluted bodies of water in the world. It is unable to renew itself because of its enclosed shape, which restricts water circulation and flushing. The sewage, plastic waste, oil runoffs, and chemical pollutants that are dumped in its waters daily cause increasing damage to the sea's fragile ecosystem. Libya has signed international agreements concerning marine dumping and wetlands preservation in an effort to protect its 1,100-mile (1,770 km) coastline from environmental pollution and contamination.

Of all the pollutants that threaten the Mediterranean Sea, oil causes the most permanent damage. Since 1983 it has been illegal to dump oil in the

Mediterranean, but tankers traveling between the Black Sea, southern Europe, North Africa, and the Middle East continue to release excess oil residues. Experts estimate that up to 363,763 tons (330,000 t) of oil are illegally dumped into the Mediterranean each year. Petroleum has many carcinogenic substances, and oil dumping causes immense damage to the tourism and fishing industries.

For centuries the people living on the Mediterranean coast have depended on the sea for survival. Libyan fishermen catch about 35,770 tons (32,450 t) of fish in the Mediterranean Sea each year, but fish populations are declining due to the high oil residue in coastal waters. Modern fishing methods such as netting have resulted in over-fishing in most areas and the marine populations are not given a chance to replenish their previously staggering numbers. Issues such as the dumping of open sewage and the harvesting of red coral for tourist curios have contributed to the decline of marine life in the Mediterranean. In recent years awareness of the sea's pollution has grown and the international community is taking action to protect its fragile waterways. The combined impact of sewage, oil by-products, and industrial waste threatens the nation's coast and the Mediterranean Sea generally. Only about 68 percent of the people living in rural areas have pure drinking water.

Floating cages full of tuna are towed from a fishing ground off the coast of Libya.

INTERNET LINKS

www.greenprophet.com/2010/06/libya-pivot-irrigation
This site shows Libya's attempt to irrigate the desert, turning wasteland into farmland.

www.temehu.com/Wild-life-in-sahara.htm
This site includes beautiful shots and descriptions of plants and animals in the Libyan Desert.

LIBYANS

A young Tuareg man wears a traditional indigo veil as protection against the wind and heat, and also to ward off evil spirits, which, according to custom, try to enter humans through the mouth.

6

ALMOST ALL LIBYANS TODAY ARE Arabic-speaking Muslims, descended from the Arabs who settled in the area during the last 1,200 years. Many of the early Arabs married into Berber families or into the families of the descendants of Roman or Greek colonists, and so few Libyans today are of pure Arab descent. Some Libyans look like Turks or Egyptians, while others have the darker skin of the desert nomads.

The native population of Libya is primarily Arab or a mixture of Arab-Berber ethnicities, with a small minority of Berber-speaking tribal groups and small African groups like Tuareg and Tebu.

Two Berber women wear traditional colorful clothing in Ghadames, an oasis town on the northwestern border of Libya.

Although the desert-separated areas of Tripolitania, Cyrenaica, and Fezzan have been one country since 1951, Libyans still tend to think tribally as well as nationally. The tribe is the basic unit of Libya's social structure and the *bayt* (bait)—the family within the tribe—is the social group to which they feel they belong.

MINORITY GROUPS

In the southern oases, there are a few communities of pure Berber ancestry. Proud of their origins, they tend to live apart from other Libyans. There are some Libyans who think of themselves as Turkish, or descendants of Turkish soldiers who settled in the area in the days of the Ottoman Empire.

Another minority group is the Sharifs, who live only in Fezzan oases and claim descent from the Prophet Muhammad. There are black Africans from Sudan and countries south of the Sahara, many of whom were originally brought to Libya as slaves. Most are now Muslims and are considered Libyans.

A few Maltese sponge fishers live on the coast. There were once small colonies of Italian farmers who settled in Libya during the Italian occupation, but they were expelled in 1970.

AFRICAN ARABS

Some say that Arabs form as much as 97 percent of Libya's population, or more than six million people, and that two-thirds of all Arabs in the world live in Africa.

Most of Libya's population is crowded in the north near the Mediterranean coast, where there is a greater chance for employment. More than 95 percent of Libyans live in Tripolitania and Cyrenaica, where they have a better quality of life and good access to government services. Fewer than 5 percent of Libyans live in Fezzan, mostly Bedouin and other groups that can survive in the harsh desert region. On the Mediterranean coastal strip, Libyans are exposed to a modern lifestyle, Western ideas, and contact with foreign workers, but they are still strongly influenced by traditional Islamic customs.

Men pray in the street in Sabha, Libya.

Many Libyan families have been farmers for generations, although few produce more than just enough for their own small community to live on.

In the cities of Tripoli and Benghazi, one can see the sharp contrast between rich and poor. Senior army officers, administrators, directors of state companies, lawyers, and foreign technical experts all live in newly built suburbs where shops sell black-market goods from abroad.

The bulk of the people live in state-built apartment buildings that are short on space, light, and hygiene. They line up for food at the state-controlled supermarkets. On the outskirts of the cities are the spreading shanty towns.

THE BEDOUIN

Deep in the Libyan Desert, there is a semi-nomadic group of people called the Bedouin. Their name means "desert dwellers" in Arabic. Their territory stretches from the vast deserts of North Africa to the rocky sands of the Middle East. Although they are divided into separate groups with their own

Dairy products are the main food source for the Bedouin. They make a kind of yogurt from camel and goat milk and also butter. Most of their meals consist of a bowl of camel or goat milk, yogurt, or rice covered with ghee, or clarified butter. They eat road loaves of unleavened bread with available with dates from oasis palm trees for dessert. Meat is a rarity eaten only on special occasions. Of course, there is no refrigeration in the Bedouin nomadic existence, so all food must be eaten fresh or otherwise preserved.

territory, the Bedouin share a common culture of herding camels and goats. They measure their wealth by the number of animals in their herd and the quality of their thoroughbred Arabian horses. Bedouins live in family groups called clans and have to move their camps several times a year to find fresh grazing lands for their herds.

For centuries the Bedouin have been known for their hospitality and courage. During medieval times they often raided caravans and desert outposts for gold and other treasure. During the Islamic Empire rulers found

A Bedouin man leads some camels.

the Bedouin impossible to control and often let them rule themselves. Even today the Bedouin enjoy a semi-autonomous existence in Libya.

Despite the Libyan government's attempts to organize the Bedouin, most prefer their traditional way of life in the desert. Even young Bedouin men who work in the cities return frequently to their camps in times of trial and celebration, and their roots remain strong.

The ruins of an ancient Berber village stand in the desert.

THE BERBERS

When the Arab invaders swept across North Africa in the seventh century, the fiercest resistance came from the northwest (now Tunisia, Algeria, and Morocco). The Arabs called the area Jazirat Al Maghreb, or "the island of the west." The inhabitants of the area were Berbers, and their descendants still live in Libya. They are believed to be the original inhabitants of North Africa.

It is thought that the Berbers, also known as the Amazigh (meaning "free men"), once inhabited the entire northern half of the African continent. After the Arab invasion, many Berbers converted to Islam.

From the eleventh to the thirteenth centuries, two Berber groups, called the Almoravids and Almohads, became powerful enough to build Islamic empires in northwestern Africa and Spain.

Now making up little more than 3 percent of the Libyan population, pure-blooded Berbers live in inaccessible mountain areas such as Jabal Nafusah and a few isolated oases in Fezzan where their ancestors retreated to escape the Arabs. They grow crops and keep herds of sheep and goats, often living a semi-nomadic life to find sufficient pasture.

This distinct culture, suppressed and oppressed by the Gaddafi regime, has risen to new prominence in the course of the 2011 war against Gaddafi, when they contributed greatly to the dictator's overthrow. Berbers consider themselves members of individual groups rather than a single nation. Most are Muslim and belong to the Kharijite sect of Islam. They revere local saints and holy places from their religious tradition. The old Berber language and their reluctance to marry out of their group have set them apart from other ethnic groups.

Berber women enjoy more personal freedom than Arab women. They had the right to own property, get a divorce, and remarry long before Muslim women gained such rights.

PEOPLE OF THE BLUE VEIL

The Tuareg are a fiercely independent desert people who do not consider themselves as belonging to any particular country. The remaining Tuareg groups are found in Libya, northwestern Niger, and Mali. Many are still nomadic, but their ancient way of life is now restricted by national borders, so most have settled around oases.

The Tuareg can be distinguished from the white-clothed Berbers by their dark blue cloaks and are known as the People of the Blue Veil. The origin of the custom of wearing a veil grew from the need for protection from sand and sun, but it is also a mark of pride. In contrast to Islamic tradition, it is the Tuareg man who veils his face; the woman is not so bound, though she will usually cover her mouth in the presence of strangers or her father-in-law. Property is inherited by children through the mother, not the father.

The population of Libya in 2015 is estimated to be 6.4 million. Life expectancy is 74.54 years for men and 78.06 years for women. Since 1965, access to improved medical care and nutrition has resulted in a decline in the death rate to 3.58 per 1,000 people. The population growth rate is 2.23 percent. The infant mortality rate in 2014 was 11.48 per 1,000 births. Estimates show that 91 percent of Libyans are literate. Libya has the highest literacy rate in northern Africa. Eighty percent of Libyans live in cities.

Like the Bedouin, the Tuareg were notorious for raiding settlements and stealing livestock. The Tuareg once achieved brief Hollywood fame as the "bad guys" in the movie *Beau Geste*. The 2005 film featured a fictionalized group of Tuareg as a faction in a civil war under way in Mali. They speak their own language, which they write in their own ancient alphabet. Part of Tuareg society are the black African *iklan* (ik-LAWN), who were originally slaves captured during raids across the Niger.

THE MODERN LIBYAN

Outspoken opposition to Gaddafi's theories of the ideal socialist Arab state were ruthlessly punished under Gaddafi's regime. Many people in the business community were arrested or had their property confiscated under the anti-corruption laws introduced in 1994. The job of confiscating assets was carried out by Purification Committees, which were made up of young military officers and students. It is also believed that hundreds of people were sent to prison for political reasons. The eastern part of the country became impoverished under Gaddafi's economic theories. At the start of the civil war, one-fifth of Libyans were unemployed, and one-third lived below the national poverty line.

Traditionally, Tuareg women wear their wealth in the form of silver jewelry. The people are famous for their silver crafts.

IMMIGRANT WORKERS

Libya's history of colonization and invasions has made Libyans suspicious of foreigners. Foreigners have at various times been banned from working in Libya. During the UN sanctions (1992—1999), Gaddafi ordered nearly all Americans and Europeans to leave the country, but after 1999 European companies were once again encouraged to invest in Libya. The suspension of sanctions by the United Nations in 1999 produced an increase in the number of foreigners working in Libya. They were valued for their expertise in technical fields, as few Libyans have such expertise. The foreigners included Italians, Germans, Britons, Thais, Koreans, and Indians. Today, however, most governments advise their citizens not to go to Libya.

WHAT TO WEAR?

For centuries style and clothing throughout the Middle East and across Africa were dictated by Islamic tradition. Men wore long white robes that kept them cool during the day. They also wore a rope-bound headscarf or wound turban. The way the turban was knotted was a clear indication of the area in which one lived. Women also wore robes to preserve their modesty, an important virtue in Islamic society. From the age of puberty, they kept their faces veiled whenever men were present, and married women often wore black to denote their marital status.

Gradually the styles of the West arrived. The red Turkish fez and European suits spread through the Mediterranean Arab world and to Libya. Apart from the Arabic posters, shop names, and road signs, there is little difference between the streets of Tripoli or Benghazi and those in almost any Mediterranean port. Girls wear bright-colored dresses, often with dark-colored trousers beneath for modesty; boys wear shirts and jeans.

College students and young married couples tend to wear modern clothes: an open-necked shirt in summer, a turtleneck in winter, with a leather jacket or zipped parka for men. Women still wear a headscarf, even with a blouse and skirt.

Traditional dresses are long and flowing, and worn with charms and necklaces that are believed to protect the wearer from evil spells. Qur'anic verses are also worn around the neck. Army uniforms are visible, as are modern suits with shirt and tie and traditional Arab robes for older people. Young men go bareheaded; others wear a black or white Islamic cap.

South of the coastal cities, people wear the Arab robes of Islamic tradition. The robes are white, loose, and flowing, and are more comfortable to wear in the hot desert climate because they trap the wind and reflect the sunlight.

Most Libyans dress in modern clothes, like these children in a refugee camp during the civil war.

INTERNET LINKS

www.temehu.com/imazighen/berbers.htm
Here, find a complete history of the Berbers of North Africa.

www.temehu.com/Libyan-People.htm
This site gives a comprehensive view of the people of Libyan from a tribal point of view.

LIFESTYLE

A boy rollerskates in the capital city in 2014.

7

W EALTH FROM THE OIL INDUSTRY brought social challenges as the income gap between the rich and poor widened dramatically. However, one thing that did not change was religion. Islam remains central to Libya's way of life.

Both scripture and tradition bind Islamic life in Libya. Families in Libya dress mainly in traditional clothes. They attend the mosque regularly, and each day is structured around the five prayer times. People stay close to home in the evening. No one goes out for a drink. Alcohol is forbidden, and there are no bars or nightclubs. Friday is the Islamic holy day, as Saturday is for Jews and Sunday for Christians. Muslims go to the mosque at noon on Fridays to join in public prayer and on other days if time permits.

However, the Libyan way of life in urban areas along the coast is modern and liberal when compared to the centuries-old lifestyle inland. Working in the fields or tending the animals is considered a reward in itself. People in those areas have been forced to live that way not because of religion but because of the environment.

HOMES

The traditional home of a prosperous Libyan family is built to an accepted pattern. Behind a stout wooden door is a corridor leading to a bright patio. The rooms of the house are grouped around this open-air square, which often has a pool or fountain in the middle. The square is the focal point for family activities. The rooms have plain, whitewashed walls, but

the floors are decorated with carpets and tasseled cushions on low benches. Some houses also have intricately designed tiles and ceilings.

The days of such lavish styles, which go back to the days of the Umayyad Empire in the eighth century, are passing. Most city-dwellers live in apartment buildings. Color-washed walls are cheaper than Persian carpets, though families like to have rugs if they can afford them. A low couch along one wall is common, and embroidered cushions take the place of armchairs. The kitchen area is traditionally the woman's private domain.

Farther inland, many houses are built of mud bricks. Mud walls are perfectly suited to the desert climate because they keep the house cool during summer and trap warm air during the coldest months of winter.

Most houses have only one floor, with a flat roof and sometimes molded pinnacles on each corner. They have very small windows—partly for privacy and partly because the walls are stronger that way. Fancier homes in the cities are built around a central courtyard. Narrow alleyways between the houses provide shade.

A WOMAN'S PLACE

Islamic society is patriarchal—families are headed by the father. For years in Libya, only boys went to school. No one could see any point in educating girls, who were expected to become wives and mothers.

In Libya women have had the right to vote and run for public office since 1963, but few choose to do so. Gaddafi tried to change the inferior status of women by passing legislation that gives them equal rights. They have access to education and employment, but most choose jobs dominated by women such as nursing, teaching, social work, and secretarial work. Islamic law in Libya denies women custody of children, alimony payments, and equal inheritance after divorce.

A Libyan woman displays her voter ID card at a polling station in Benghazi in 2014.

It is very important in Libyan society for women to be modest. Only a woman's hands, feet, and face may be left uncovered in public, and to disregard these conventions is a serious offence against family honor. Within an Arab group, a man's reputation depends largely on the behavior of the women in his family. Most girls start wearing the traditional black cloak and veil at puberty, but in some families even six-year-old girls cover their heads.

Many Libyan women now work outside the home. Raising children and taking care of the house remain women's responsibilities, however, and most women in Libya stay home at least when their children are very young. More traditional families restrict a woman's outdoor movements to only the most essential activities. Before the revolution, working mothers enjoyed a range of benefits designed to encourage them to continue working even after marriage and childbirth, including cash bonuses for the first child and free daycare centers. A woman could retire at age fifty-five, and she was entitled to a pension. The revolution launched in February 2011 turned life in Libya upside-down. Retail sales dropped amid the uncertainty, and some

A young boy carries empty containers to fill with clean water as Tripoli struggles with water shortages in 2011.

shop owners in battle-scarred towns don't even bother to roll up their metal store shutters in the morning. The Libyan dinar is depreciating, with $1 trading at 1.85 dinars or more on the black market, compared with the official 1.37-dinar-per-dollar exchange rate (2015).

Prices for staples such as noodles, tea, and milk are up, and the cost of a pack of cigarettes has more than doubled, a major irritant in a nation where smoking is commonplace. Inventories in shops have thinned, and those who live within driving distance of the Tunisian border stock up there.

Men, the traditional breadwinners, left for the frontline or lost their jobs, universities and schools closed, and businesses and homes were hit by daily power cuts. Women have left their homes to look for jobs.

CHILDREN

Children are extremely valued in Libya and throughout the Arab world. Most people cannot imagine life without marriage and many children. Traditionally, the birth of a woman's first child raised her status to that of a full-fledged member of the community, but that is changing as more women seek employment and fulfillment outside the home.

Most Muslim babies have their heads shaved because of religious custom, and male babies are circumcised. However, sometimes the family decides to wait and incorporates the circumcision into an important ceremony when the boy is ten or eleven years old.

Libyan children grow up accepting that all important decisions will be made by their father. In general, children in the Arab world—especially in rural areas—have much more responsibility than children in the West. Although they have some time to play and joke with their young relatives and friends, they help with household chores and often take care of their younger siblings. They are treated as small adults, expected to help the family once they are no longer toddlers. In Fezzan families, young girls care for the babies while their mother is out, milk the goats, and fetch water from the well.

Before his fall from power, Colonel Gaddafi always had a posse of all-female bodyguards with him. The group was formed in the early 1980s. They had the unofficial name of the "Amazonian Guard," given by Western journalists, but were officially known as "The Revolutionary Nuns."

Gaddafi would usually travel with fifteen of his young female guards, who were assigned to protect the dictator from harm and also to do housekeeping for him. The women had to take a vow of chastity and pledge to give up their life for their leader.

All of the women underwent extensive training in the use of firearms and techniques of martial arts at a special academy. In 1998, one of the female bodyguards was killed and seven others were wounded when Gaddafi's motorcade was attacked.

EDUCATION

School is free and compulsory in Libya for children aged six to fifteen. Lessons are taught exclusively in Arabic. Besides Arabic, schoolchildren study the Qur'an and Islamic teaching and traditions. The syllabus for older children includes other subjects such as history, geography, and science.

Libyan boys attend special religious classes after school. They listen to the Qur'an being recited and memorize the verses. A few private schools cater to children from wealthy families.

Libyans can further their education at the established universities of Garyounis in Benghazi and Al Fatah in Tripoli or at the new universities

in Sabha and Marsa al Burayqah. There are also agricultural, technical, and vocational training institutes. In 1951, nearly 90 percent of the Libyan population was illiterate. There were no girls in the intermediate and high schools. By 2015, an estimated 89.5 percent of the population could now read and write. The estimated literacy rate of the female population was 83.3 percent in 2011.

MARRIAGE

Students attend English class as the school reopens for the first time in seven months during the Libyan civil war in 2011.

According to Islamic law, a man can have up to four wives at one time, but he must provide each with equal possessions and give each an equal amount of his time. Today most Libyans marry only once.

In spite of the modern trend toward marrying for love, most Libyan marriages are still arranged by the couple's parents. However, the couples often know each other before the wedding. Family connections, social class, education, and employment status all count in choosing a spouse.

The marriage ceremony in the Arab world does not take place in a mosque. Instead, the mosque's cleric, or imam, goes to the groom's house to write out the marriage contract. Once the document is signed, family and friends rejoice, dance, and sing. The bride is led to her husband's house in a joyous procession. Celebrations continue with a huge banquet.

In Islam, marriage is a religious duty and children are considered a blessing from God. For the Bedouin, marriage was a means of strengthening connections and forming alliances between families.

In traditional Islamic law, a husband is allowed to divorce his wife by saying "I divorce you" three times in front of two witnesses. Since 1973 women have had equal rights in obtaining a divorce, but they have been reluctant to use

The ancient traditions of Bedouin hospitality arise from the harsh conditions of the desert. The Bedouin believe that if a stranger comes to their tent dying of thirst, they should give the stranger food and shelter for three days, even if the stranger might have murdered a member of their family.

Bedouin hosts brew fresh coffee for their guests and the family drinks whatever is left later. They use beautiful brass jugs that may be among the family's most prized possessions to serve their guests. In the cities, people offer their guests a cup of tea or coffee. Owners of traditional shops do the same for their customers, but the practice does not fit the fast-paced supermarket culture of the cities.

Although the Bedouin regard hospitality as a duty and offer it freely to any visitor, they guard their honor fiercely and jealously. Upholding honor may mean death, as an insult can start a blood feud. Robbery and theft are not common in Bedouin society. People respect one another's property, and a Bedouin family can safely leave their rolled-up tent weighted with stones on the ground without worry of it being stolen while they are away.

it because of the social stigma it brings. Nevertheless, divorce is now more socially accepted in the Arab world, and it is common for both the man and woman to remarry.

HEALTH

Gaddafi's socialist government instituted free health services and increased facilities dramatically. In comparison to other states in the Middle East, the

At the Al-Zawiya Hospital in 2011, Libyan nurses treat a wounded National Transitional Council fighter.

health status of the population is relatively good. Childhood immunization is almost universal. Clean water supply has increased and sanitation has been improved.

There are two large hospitals, in Tripoli and Benghazi, and many smaller hospitals and clinics around the country, while mobile health units visit the country districts. However, many of these facilities have been damaged by the civil war.

Some schools provide health services and supplement the children's diet, and there were some mother-and-child care centers. Instead of the Red Cross, there are clinics run by the Red Crescent Society as it is called in Islamic countries. However, traditions that prevent married women from coming into contact with any man other than their husband have made it hard for Libyan women to be trained as nurses or doctors.

Malaria has been wiped out with the aid of the World Health Organization, and significant progress was made against trachoma (an eye disease that can lead to blindness) and leprosy. However, a drug-resistant strain of tuberculosis has emerged.

DEATH AND BURIAL

Libyan children are brought up not to be frightened by the idea of death. Muslims believe that everything comes from God and, however difficult the circumstances may be, everything happens for the best. It is considered holy to face life's trials calmly and without complaint. Certainly the Bedouin meet death all too often in the harsh desert.

Relatives carry the coffin of a victim of shelling by the Gaddafi forces in Misrata in 2011.

No Libyan family would ever put an elderly relative into an old age home. They are glad to have elderly family members at home, where they can turn to them for advice. With their family around them, the elderly accept the approach of death in a dignified manner. A Libyan might well gather friends and relatives and say farewell to each one before he or she dies.

According to tradition, the dead body is washed in water or sand. It is then clothed in fresh linen and buried in a shallow grave. The custom is to lay the corpse facing Mecca. In the desert, few people attend this ceremony. In the towns, many do, anxious to help carry the body. Women are not allowed to be part of the funeral procession because it is believed that they are too emotional. Extreme or exaggerated expressions of grief are not allowed in Islam. For ordinary people, no monuments or headstones are used. Muslims believe that once a person is dead, the body is of no further use.

INTERNET LINKS

www.ft.com/cms/s/0/eec110b6-ffd4-11e4-abd5-00144feabdc0.html#axzz3n9zthzA8
This article from *Financial Times* offers insight into how the current violence in Libya is affecting everyday life.

www.funeralwise.com/customs/islam
This site provides a look at Islamic death and burial customs.

RELIGION

The Bilal bin Rabah Mosque in Al Bayda, Libya, is an example of Islamic architecture.

SLAM IS MUCH MORE THAN A RELIGION; it is a way of life. It determines all aspects of a Muslim's life, from marriage to food to family life to the structure of society. It is undoubtedly the most important force in shaping Libyan life and society.

Libyan men pray in Martyr's Square in Tripoli as they mark the Eid al-Adha holiday.

8

"He who helps a Muslim in his worldly distress will be rewarded by Allah on the day of judgment."
—the Prophet Muhammad

The religion of Libya is Islam. The word Islam means "submission to the will of Allah." Allah is the word Muslims use for God, who is considered compassionate and merciful but cannot be fully known. Islam is divided into two sects: about 90 percent of the world's total Muslim population is made up of members of the Sunni sect; the rest belong to the Shi'ite sect. Most Libyans are Sunni Muslims. The Sunni branch of Islam provides both a spiritual guide for individuals and a keystone for government policy. Its tenets stress a unity of religion and state rather than a separation or distinction between the two, and even those Muslims who have ceased to believe fully in Islam retain Islamic habits and attitudes.

Since the 1969 revolution, everything Arabic and Islamic in Libya has been intensified, while anything considered contrary to Islamic beliefs is destroyed or forbidden. Gaddafi strongly encouraged conversions to Islam in African countries such as Nigeria.

SHARI'AH LAW

Although the country today is split between the rule of two governments and a variety of armed groups, everyday life in Libya continues to be ruled by the sacred law of Islam is called Shari'ah (SHARI-ya). Shari'ah means "the path of Allah's commandments." Allah is the Arabic word for "God." Shari'ah is sometimes summarized as:

- what God has commanded
- what God has recommended
- what God has left for us to choose
- what God disapproves of
- what God has forbidden

The Shari'ah courts deal with family matters and business and property claims. Islamic law, if fully enforced, threatens such punishments as the amputation of a thief's hands.

There is also a criminal code of justice in Libya based mainly on the Egyptian model that has judges and a court of appeal. However, all family matters are settled according to Shari'ah law, which originates from the Qur'an.

THE PROPHET MUHAMMAD

The Prophet Muhammad, the founder of Islam, was born in Mecca, a prosperous trading town in what is now Saudi Arabia, in 570 CE, more than five centuries after the birth of Jesus Christ. After Muhammad's father died, his mother could not afford to look after him, so he was sent to live with his grandfather in the desert. He started as a herd boy and later worked for his uncle, traveling with the camel caravans. At the age of twenty-five, he married a woman named Khadija, who became one of his staunchest supporters. They had six children, but the Muhammad's surviving descendants were all the children of his daughter, Fatimah.

As Muhammad traveled, he became aware of Judaism and Christianity. He also knew that many people in Arabia still worshiped idols. He traveled into the mountains, where he began to have dreams and visions. Muslims believe that while he was in the mountains, Muhammad heard the words of God spoken to him by the angel Gabriel. Although Muhammad himself could not read or write, he told others what he had heard. The words were written down and became the holy book of Islam, the Qur'an.

Muslims enter the Holy Mosque in Mecca through the King al Fahad Gate.

When the Prophet Muhammad took his words to Mecca in the hope that people there would turn to Allah, he met with fierce opposition. In 622 CE, preceded by about seventy men and their families, he migrated to a town farther north, called Medina, where the people welcomed his arrival. There, he built the first mosque.

By 629 CE, after years of fierce fighting between the two towns, Muhammad's support was strong enough for him to lead his forces into Mecca. The square enclosure that had once housed idols became the sacred Ka'bah (kah-AH-bah), the central shrine of pilgrimage for Muslims.

Muhammad died in 632 CE and was buried at Medina. Muslims don't worship Muhammad, but he is respected and honored as God's last prophet.

THE FIVE PILLARS OF ISLAM

Every Muslim accepts five basic religious duties:

1. Shahada(sha-HAD-ah)—the confession of faith. This means to bear witness that there is no god other than Allah and that the Prophet Muhammad is his final messenger and prophet.

2. Salat (sahl-AHT)—prayer. This means to pray five times daily, facing the direction of Mecca, at daybreak, noon, mid-afternoon, after sunset, and early in the night.

3. Zakat (za-KAHT)—alms giving. This refers to giving 2.5 percent of one's annual earnings to the poor and needy.

4. Fasting during the month of Ramadan (rah-mah-DAHN). Muslims go without food or drink between dawn and sunset for the thirty days of the lunar month.

5. Hajj—pilgrimage. This refers to making the pilgrimage to Mecca once in a lifetime.

Muslims also have six main beliefs at the foundation of their faith. They believe that Allah is the only God and that there exist angels, holy books, prophets, the Day of Judgment, and pre-destiny.

SHI'ISM

Shi'ites make up the second-largest Islamic sect in Libya. Shi'a Muslims broke away from the dominant Sunnis for reasons of theology and politics. One difference stems from arguments over the Prophet Muhammad's successors as caliphs, the spiritual leaders of Muslims. The Shi'ites wanted the caliphate to descend through Ali, the Prophet Muhammad's son-in-law. Ali eventually became the fourth caliph, but he was murdered soon after. Since then, the Shi'ites have accused the later caliphs, whom the Sunnis followed, of being usurpers.

Shi'ites also regard their holy men as having far greater authority than ordinary Muslims. This opposes the Sunni belief that their religious leaders are ordinary Muslims who have received extra training as teachers and leaders in prayer.

PLACE OF PRAYER

A mosque is a place of worship, as is a church. Indeed, many buildings have been used as one and then the other. Structurally, the greatest difference is that a Christian worshipper usually enters a church at one end of the building to see the altar at the far end, whereas a Muslim more often enters the mosque in the middle of one of the long walls and faces across.

Although churches were traditionally built with the altar at the eastern end (for most of Europe, the eastern end pointed to Jerusalem, where Jesus was crucified and resurrected), mosques are oriented so that worshipers directly face Mecca, the sacred city of Islam.

Every mosque needs a tower from which the muezzin, or mosque official, can give the call to prayer. Often the towers are in the shape of a slender minaret, with hundreds of steps leading to the top. Today, a muezzin usually uses a loudspeaker system, made essential by the clamor of the modern city. The muezzin was once chosen from among the blind, so that they could

The beautiful interior of the Jami Gurgi Mosque in the old Medina section of Tripoli attracts many tourists.

concentrate on the prayer and not be distracted by the view from the top of the minaret.

A running fountain in the courtyard is also an essential facility for worshippers because Islam prescribes that people cleanse themselves with water before they pray. Some mosques even have a bathhouse, similar to a Turkish bath, attached.

WITHIN THE BUILDING

To people who are used to ornate, furnished Christian churches, a mosque may seem empty. Whether large or small, the mosque is essentially an open space covered with carpets for the kneeling worshipers.

There are only two particular features. In the eastern wall is an empty recess called the *mihrab* (mi-RAHB), which indicates the direction of Mecca. There is also the *minbar* (MIN-bar), or pulpit, often in the shape of a narrow flight of steps, from which the imam leads prayers and preaches.

No images or pictures adorn the walls or pillars because Islam forbids the depiction of living creatures, but mosques are often resplendent with artistic shapes, colorful tiles, geometric designs, and Arabic calligraphy.

The decorated walls, the rich carpets, the stained-glass windows, and the architectural symmetry all combine to contribute to an atmosphere of holy splendor.

PILGRIMAGE TO MECCA

Once a small desert town visited only by caravans of camels, Mecca is now a major city in Saudi Arabia. It is the holiest place of Islam. It had some importance even before the birth of the Prophet Muhammad. A black stone, probably a meteorite, was said to have been sent by God. The black stone was built into the wall of a square enclosure that housed a profusion of idols. That square building is the Ka'bah. Today it is draped with a ceremonial black cloth embroidered with gold called the *kiswah* (KEYS-wa). The Great Mosque has been built around the Ka'bah.

Islamic tradition frowns on superstition. Nevertheless, Muslims pay great attention to dreams, which they believe are sent by God. In many communities there are people known for their ability to interpret dreams. Most Libyans believe that dreams have an opposite result. For example, a frightening dream may well be a good sign. Dreams can also be warnings of dire happenings, although such events cannot be avoided—they are "the will of Allah."

Muslims believe that sickness may be sent by God, or through the power of a curse from someone wishing another harm. Many Libyans wear charms, usually a small container with a verse from the Qur'an, on a leather thong. Some pregnant women wear an earring in the shape of a blue hand with an eye on its palm. The hand is called the khamsa *(KHAHM-sa), or the hand of Fatimah, and is meant to protect the wearer from harm and bad luck.*

Some older Libyans believe in the existence of evil spirits called jinn that live in haunted places. They can drive a person insane or kill them. Jinn are believed to be able to assume the form of snakes, dogs, cats, monsters, or people.

Mecca is now an endlessly crowded town among sheltering hills. Muslim pilgrims on their annual pilgrimage are expected to camp in the desert as the Prophet Muhammad once did, but that has not prevented Mecca from becoming a town of hotels and souvenir shops. Traffic is an increasing problem, and there are plans to build elevated bypass roads. Visitors arrive by air or through the adjoining port of Jiddah on the Red Sea.

GENIES AND SPELLS

Strict Muslims like to hear stories from the Qur'an and about the life of the Prophet Muhammad. Many Libyans also enjoy listening to folktales passed down for many generations that tell of enchanted lands and the spirit world. Many of the fables have a hero who encounters a genie or another type of magical creature that helps him win his fortune. The hero also often meets mythical creatures, such as winged monsters, and wicked sorcerers who cast evil spells. Although such stories are frowned upon by strict Islamic tradition, they are very popular with Libyans.

FOOD AND FASTING

An essential principle of Islam is submission to God, and a Muslim's diet must also conform to the will of God. In Libya, the Islamic diet is strictly observed. Alcohol is forbidden in any form. Visitors are not allowed to bring alcohol into Libya, whether or not they are Muslim. As in Judaism, pork products are also forbidden, as the pig is not considered a "clean" animal.

Fasting is also part of the discipline imposed by the faith. The word breakfast reminds us that, after a night without food or drink, we break our fast in the morning. All over the Islamic world, Ramadan is the holy month of fasting. The time of Ramadan changes each year. In 2015, it was from June 15 to July 15. In 2016, it will begin on June 6 and end on July 5. During the holy month, Muslims are not allowed food or water each day from sunrise to sunset. The fast is broken after evening prayers are completed, when the family comes together for a large meal. Non-Muslim visitors to Libya are obliged to respect the fast during Ramadan.

MINORITY RELIGIONS IN LIBYA

Christianity has been a minority religion in Libya since the Arab invasions. The largest Christian group in Libya is the Egyptian Coptic Orthodox church, with a population of more than 60,000. Libya had the largest proportion of Buddhists of any North African country, with 0.3 percent of its population identifying itself as Buddhist.

Gaddafi stressed the universal applicability of Islam, but he also reaffirmed the special status assigned by the Prophet Muhammad to Christians. However, he likened them to misguided Muslims who have strayed from the correct path. Furthermore, he assumed leadership of a drive to free Africa of Christianity as well as of the colonialism with which it has been associated.

In 2011, a priest stands in the only Coptic church in the Misrata region of Libya. The church was later bombed, in December 2012.

Every year, about three million Muslims, including many Libyans, make the pilgrimage to Mecca in Saudi Arabia. To make this journey is an honor, a blessing, and the greatest longing of any Muslim.

Enormous camps surround Mecca at the time of the pilgrimage. Everyone wears similar clothing, so there is no distinction between rich and poor. Men wear two pieces of seamless white cloth, one wrapped around the lower body, the other draped over the shoulder. Women wear green underclothes and a cloak and veil.

The first task immediately after arrival in Mecca is to walk around the walls of the Great Mosque. Then the pilgrims join the throng inside the mosque to walk seven times around the Ka'bah. If possible, they kiss the black stone built into its outside wall, said to be a stone on which Abraham once stood. Next is the visit to drink from the sacred well of Zamzam, where prayers and ceremonials are recited.

On the eighth day, the pilgrims move to the Mount of Mercy, about 13 miles (21 km) from Mecca. There Muhammad once gave a famous sermon. The pilgrims stand or sit in meditation from midday to sunset. The shelter of an umbrella is permitted if the hajj falls during the intense heat of summer. This visit is considered so important that if it is omitted the pilgrimage is considered to have no value.

At sunset they move to Mina to throw stones at three stone pillars representing the devil. In Muhammad's time, the three pillars belonged to a popular temple for goddess worship that was demolished when he returned with his followers to Mecca.

On the tenth day the end of the hajj is marked by the great Feast of Sacrifice. It is a time for giving alms, for prayers and rejoicing, for sermons in the open air, and for the sacrifice of a lamb, goat, cow, or camel. The feast officially lasts three days, but the celebrations often continue for a full week.

Each pilgrim washes, cuts off ceremonial locks of hair, and puts on new clothes to symbolize the entering of a new life. Some pilgrims go back to the Ka'bah after that for a farewell circling. Before leaving Saudi Arabia, the pilgrim may visit Medina, where Muhammad built his first mosque and where he is buried.

The return of the pilgrims is another cause for celebrations. Many Libyans paint their houses with murals of the pilgrimage, and their neighbors come to congratulate them.

INTERNET LINKS

www.islam.com
This is a site covering a wide range of topics and issues relating to Islam today.

www.metmuseum.org/learn/for-educators/publications-for-educators/art-of-the-islamic-world/unit-one/the-prophet-muhammad-and-the-origins-of-islam
This is an educational website on Islam from the Metropolitan Museum of Art.

news.discovery.com/history/religion/fragments-of-worlds-oldest-Qur'an-may-predate-muhammad-150901.htm
This article discuess the world's oldest Qur'an, which may actually predate the Prophet Mohammad.

www.pbs.org/wgbh/pages/frontline/teach/terror/background/6.html
PBS *Frontline* outlines basic facts about Islam.

LANGUAGE

A Libyan boy reads the Qur'an at a mosque in Tripoli.

A LTHOUGH ARABIC ORIGINATED IN A small area of the Arabian Peninsula, it is now spoken by over 150 million people around the world. It is the official language of Libya.

Arabic belongs to the Afro-Asiatic family of languages and is further classified as a Semitic language. Semites are people from the Middle East who are popularly believed to have descended from Shem, Noah's eldest son. The Semitic languages are spoken in North Africa and the Middle East. Besides Arabic, this group of languages includes Hebrew, Amharic, and the ancient language of Aramaic, the original language of Palestine. Modern spoken Arabic has regional differences, but most Arabic-speaking countries use standard Arabic, based on the language of the Qur'an, in their books and newspapers.

The National Archives holds an extensive collection of historical documents dating from Ottoman rule.

ANCIENT AFRICA

The most ancient language of Libya is the Numidian language of the Berbers that is still spoken in isolated places in Jabal Nafusah. A modified form of this language remains in *tifinagh* (tee-fee-nawkh), the geometrical alphabet used by the Tuareg. Most Libyan Berbers, however, have adopted Arabic.

GADDAFI AND THE BERBERS

The Berber minority in Libya suffered great oppression and discrimination under Gaddafi's rule. Gaddafi refused to acknowledge the Berbers as a people and culture and used Arabization as a means to achieve nationalism. He was particularly disdainful of their language, Tamazight. Berber towns were renamed and it was considered illegal for children to be given Berber names until 2009. Schools were not allowed to teach the Berber language. Despite being able to speak Berber, many young Berbers had never seen their language in its written form, much less understood it. This oppression and destruction of their language and identity was part of the reason that Berbers were willing to join in the fight against Gaddafi's rule.

Gaddafi's policies heralded the demise of Tamazight, with people fearful of the repercussions of teaching, using, or promoting the language and culture. But the death of Gaddafi signaled new hope for the Berbers and the continuation of their language and culture. However, it will be difficult to change the mindsets of the predominantly Arab-speaking population. Previous Arab conquest heralded Arabic as the language of God and stigmatized the use of Tamazight. Berber identity has often been overlooked in favor of nationalism, a call for a unified Libya.

ARABIC WORDS

In the years when Muslim traders sailed to the shores of the Mediterranean, many European languages adopted words from Arabic. Many places in Arab countries have Arabic names beginning with Al, meaning "the." English words such as alcohol, almanac, alfalfa, alcove, and algebra come from Arabic. Here are some others: admiral, coffee, giraffe, caravan, lemon, kebab, and marzipan.

Words with connected meanings in Arabic often contain the same pattern of consonants. For example, s-l-m is the root of words such as *salaam* (meaning "peace"), *Islam*, and *Muslim*.

ARABIC AND THE QUR'AN

Among the earliest teachings of Islam was the necessity for Muslims to be taught to read. Only then could they read the Qur'an.

Since all Muslims are required to study the Qur'an, all Muslims must also learn Arabic, because the Qur'an should be read in Arabic. Muslims believe that the Qur'an would not truly reflect the word of God in any other language. That is why Arabic is the official spoken and written language of Libya. But because there are many specialists from the Western world working in Libya, other languages such as English and Italian are spoken by some.

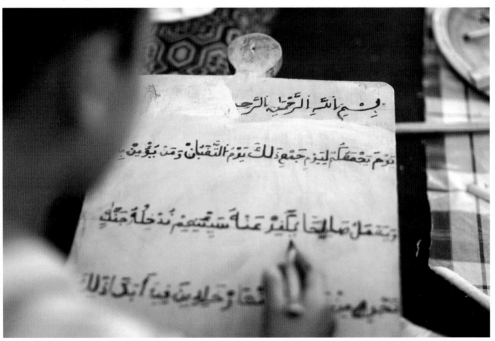

A Libyan child writes on a slate as he memorizes the Qur'an at a religious school in Tripoli.

THE LANGUAGE OF CHESS

In chess, a game adopted by Christian Europe from the Islamic world, several terms we use today come from the Arabic or Persian languages. The word checkmate comes from the Persian shah mat, *meaning, "the king is dead." The castle is also called the rook, which comes from the Persian* rukh. *The word rook can also mean "chariot;" the castle/rook moves in a similar straight and powerful manner. The bishop in Arabic is called* al-Fil, *"the elephant."*

The word Allah is constantly on the lips of Muslims. It is considered polite to refer to Allah often in conversation. "Praise Allah," "By Allah's permission," and "Allah is great" are as common in conversation as "good-bye." Even a simple matter such as agreeing to meet a friend at a certain time will be marked by the phrase "insh-allah," or "if Allah wills it."

VISUAL BEAUTY

Arabic was originally written in brush strokes, and its letters still look as if they have been painted rather than printed. The early editions of the Qur'an were handwritten and are beautiful to look at. Calligraphers used to be held in high regard, largely because there was no printing in the Islamic world until the eighteenth century.

Muslims are forbidden to depict God in pictures, but they love to describe him in picturesque words. Therefore, Arabic calligraphy is one of their primary art forms. In the past, because most calligraphers and their readers knew the Qur'an by heart, beautiful lettering became more important than legibility.

ARABIC NUMERALS

The number system used for centuries by the Christian world was invented by the Romans and is still known as Roman numerals. In this system, different letters stand for numbers. C stands for a hundred and M for a thousand, because they are the first letters of the Latin words *centum* and *mille*. So, for the number two thousand, two hundred, and twenty-two, the Romans wrote MMCCXXII.

How much simpler it is for people today to write 2,222. Although each figure 2 looks the same, it stands for a different amount according to its position in the number. That is because we use Arabic numerals. The Arabs, who probably borrowed the system from India about two hundred years earlier, introduced this number system to Spain at the end of the tenth century.

It took another five hundred years for the rest of Europe to accept this new system. Thanks to the Arabs, the European world was introduced to the use of the digit 0. Without this symbol, the invention of decimals would have been impossible.

Interestingly, it was Caliph Haroun al-Raschid (made famous in the Arabian Nights stories, though he was a very real person) who did much to spread mathematical ideas. He had many old Greek books translated into Arabic, including Euclid's *Elements on Mathematics* in 1482.

Arabs were also skilled astronomers. Astronomical terms such as zenith and nadir come from Arabic. Arabs knew enough about astronomy and geography to calculate the circumference and diameter of Earth. After all, it was from "the East"—perhaps Persia and the Arabian Desert—that the Three Wise Men followed the star to Bethlehem to visit the infant Jesus Christ.

IN CONVERSATION

Even non-Arabic-speaking Muslims constantly encounter the classical Arabic language in their daily prayers, the reading of the Qur'an, and in Arabic writings. God is constantly invoked in conversation, and sayings such as "in the name of God," "thanks be to God," and "may God be with you" are common expressions. *Inshallah*, meaning "if Allah wills it," is used in various situations, from a polite refusal to sealing an agreement. The Qur'an is written in classical Arabic, an old-fashioned form of the language. Fortunately now Modern Standard Arabic is used in nearly all written and printed material in Arab countries.

Traditional manners require a series of questions, each with its proper answer, when inquiring about another's health and family. Hands are clasped until the ritual questions have been answered. Important conversations are always accompanied by coffee. It would be the height of bad manners to begin a serious discussion before the pot was finished.

The normal Libyan greeting is *Salaam aleikum* ("peace be with you"), to which the correct reply is *Aleikum as-salaam* ("and also with you"). Another typical greeting is *Sabbahakum Allah bi'l-khair* ("Allah give you a good morning").

In Libya it is extremely rude to criticize someone to his or her face, so when disagreements occur, family and friends are often brought in to mediate. Tradition demands courtesy in public, and family matters are considered strictly private. Women are never discussed in public, especially not by name. Women may discuss the men in their friends' families, but among men, it is considered immodest and vulgar to mention the women in a man's family.

Gestures form a significant part of any good conversation. "No" is often accompanied with a click of the tongue and a toss of the head. Among the Tuareg, a normal greeting includes letting one's palm slide gently across the other person's and then pulling the hand back to touch the chest.

IN THE MEDIA

All forms of public entertainment in Libya were restricted to the accepted agenda prescribed by Islam. Many expressions of Western culture, including some books, films, magazines, posters, and Christian institutions, were forbidden or viewed with disapproval under Gaddafi. Ever since Arabic became the official language in 1969, all street signs, advertisements, and shop names must be written in Arabic. Speaking languages such as English and Italian in public is discouraged.

Radios, television sets, and satellite dishes are easy to purchase in Libya, and most families own one or the other. The state both owns and controls the media, and under Gaddafi's rule, the censors were quick to edit or cut programs that they saw as threatening moral values, demeaning Libya, or glorifying the West. The government ran Libya's two radio stations.

When Libya's national television station was launched in 1968, it was the only channel available in the country. With the advent of satellite technology, however, those who could afford it enjoyed wider access to international programming. Stations that broadcast in Arabic, such as the news channel Al-Jazeera and the Egyptian-run Nile TV, which even has an Arabic version of *Sesame Street*, remain popular.

The 2011 uprising saw the emergence of media outlets affiliated with opponents of Colonel Gaddafi. They include radio stations in areas wrested from the regime's control, and Libya TV—a Qatar-based satellite station. The rebels run a number of newspapers and websites. By 2014, there were 1,362,604 Internet users in Libya. Web filtering was selective, focusing on political opposition websites. Social media have served as a battleground for supporters and foes of the former regime.

An Al-Jazeera TV journalist delivers a live report from Libya during the joyous celebrations of rebels in Benghazi in 2011.

INTERNET LINKS

www.arabacademy.com/arabic-blog/arabic-language/history-of-the-arabic-language
This site tells the story of the spread of the Arabic language.

www.quora.com/Why-are-most-Semitic-languages-written-from-right-to-left-while-European-languages-are-written-left-to-right
This site attempts to answer the question about why Arabic and other Semitic languages are written from right to left instead of left to right.

ARTS

Islamic art expresses a love of pattern and design, as shown on this traditional tile work.

10

ARTS IN LIBYA TODAY BELONG TO A long tradition of Islamic art that has produced some of the world's most beautiful buildings and decorative art.

CAVE PAINTINGS

The art found in Libya are rock paintings. In Fezzan, an Italian expedition found a series of rock paintings that are more than five thousand years old. Some are painted solid red or black, others in a scraped style resembling rock engraving.

The ancient rock engravings of Tadrart Acacus depict life in a pre-Saharan time in Libya. The cave art is a **UNESCO** World Heritage site.

Blue tile work is a favorite design motif in Islamic art.

Although less spectacular, the rock paintings must have a similar origin to the rock art discovered in Algeria's Tassili N'ajjer, which is located near the Libyan border. The oldest rock paintings depict the Sahara as a green pasture with people hunting elephants, antelopes, and giraffes. The whole history of the Sahara is portrayed in the paintings at Tassili N'ajjer. After the hunters came cattle herders such as the Fulani in Nigeria. Then came paintings of chariots and horses, almost Cretan in style. Lastly, dated to about 100 BCE, there are pictures of people and camels, a clear indication of the changing geography of the Sahara.

AN INSTINCT FOR ORNAMENT

Examining Islamic art, one becomes convinced that Muslim artists hated blank space. But they never made "art for art's sake." Decoration was used to beautify everyday life, so carpets, pottery, windows, fountains, and houses became canvases for Muslim artists.

Libyan crafts once included inlaid metalwork, pottery with the glazed tiles called faience, leather work, weaving, and embroidery. However, many craft shops have disappeared since Gaddafi encouraged nationalized production. Traditional Berber designs feature zigzags and triangles, often in earthy colors of rust brown and dark blue. Arab patterns use more flowing, floral shapes known as arabesques.

THEMES

Islamic tradition favors abstract patterns and elaborate scroll work, often starkly geometric against a dark background. The polygon is the most common shape. It is easy to see that Muslim artists admired bees with their hexagonal cells for honey, and spiders with star-shaped, concentric webs. Flowers are popular, too, often portrayed as circles or decorated segments.

Muslims believe that anything created by God is perfect and that it would be wrong to copy the sublime in an imperfect way, so there can be no human figures in pictures, sculpture, decorations, or designs in mosques. To make a carving or painting of a human being that can be admired would be like making an idol to be worshiped in a mosque. Instead, Libyan artists and architects use intricate patterns of geometric designs or flowers. However, outside of mosques, depictions of people are welcomed.

CARPETS

The origin of the knotted pile rug is lost in time, but certainly the method was invented somewhere in the Middle East, quite possibly in Turkey. It seems likely that these precious and artistic possessions were originally designed as wall hangings rather than rugs to be used underfoot.

The skill of carpet weaving probably came to Libya with the arrival of Islam. While locally made rugs are still found in Libya, the best ones are imported. The coastal city of Misratah is noted for its carpet industry. Carpet weaving has been called the highest form of art in Islam. Carpets mass-produced in Libya today bear little resemblance to the traditional masterpieces that could take women as long as a year to weave.

The most common form of carpet is the prayer rug, used by Muslims during worship. The arched design imitates the mihrab in the mosque that points in the direction of Mecca, which the worshipper must face. A Muslim will unroll a prayer rug in the street or in the desert rather than pray on "unclean" ground.

The design, following Islamic custom, features flowers or geometric patterns. These designs were inspired by a love of gardens and beauty.

MUSIC

The Prophet Muhammad himself seemed to have disapproved of music, fearing perhaps that people might enjoy it too much and forget the seriousness of life. A sanctioned form of music is the chanting of the Qur'an

A father and son celebrate the birth of the Prophet Muhammad in the Old City section of Tripoli.

by a special chanter known for his voice. Qur'anic chanting is melodious and strikingly beautiful, unaccompanied by musical instruments.

Nevertheless, Arab culture finds ways to incorporate music into daily life, and songs and music celebrate special occasions such as feasts and holidays. Arab singers are renowned for their performing abilities and love songs, which are often taken from traditional Bedouin poetry.

Considering its desert origins, it is not surprising to find that Arab music relies on the voice rather than on musical instruments, although the lyre, cane pipe, drum, and tambourine accompany the singers' voices. The drum is a major component of Arab music. People like to dance to the music, although men and women are segregated when they dance.

The old poet-singers of the Bedouin sang songs about great deeds or popular heroes, much like the wandering minstrels of medieval Europe. The words were more important than the tune. The *huda* song of the camel drivers has a rhythm that is supposed to echo the movement of the camel's feet.

Music in the Western world is based on a scale of eight notes, with half tones between five of them. Arabic music, on the other hand, has quarter tones as well—a variation that makes tunes sound mournful and exciting, exotic and beautiful.

In addition to traditional musical genres, there is a huge circulation in Libya (as there is everywhere else in the Middle East) of up-to-date North African and foreign popular music, much of which integrates geographically distant instruments and genres.

ARCHITECTURE

An Arab city may seem like a maze of jumbled buildings, but much thought actually goes into its planning. The narrow alleyways provide vital shade, reduce dust, and save space. Privacy is essential—Islamic custom ensures that no door is directly opposite another, and window sills must be at least 5 feet, 9 inches (1.7 m) above ground level. Streets may seem narrow, but they must be wide enough to allow two fully loaded camels to pass each other.

A visitor to Tripoli today will instantly see the contrast between the architect-designed, pastel-shaded villas of the rich suburbs and the shanty towns on the outskirts of the city. Stone-faced minarets rise above domed eighteenth-century mosques. Beside them are patterned gardens and courtyards. A block away will be the rubble of destroyed hovels or a high-rise apartment building. Traveling south, one sees houses and mosques built of sunbaked mud bricks. Square or with hand-smoothed pointed shapes, they are often whitewashed for a touch of coolness and durability.

A typical courtyard in a building in Medina, the old section of Tripoli

CLASSICAL RUINS

Sabratha, 40 miles (64 km) west of Tripoli, holds the remains of a splendid Roman theater that could seat five thousand people under colonnades 80 feet (24 m) high. At the front of the stage is a marble relief showing the entertainment delights of drama, comedy, dance, and music. The area that was the marketplace had shops with solid stone counters where olives and olive oil, fruit and grain, hides and ivory, and live birds and slaves were sold to Rome.

Even more splendid was Leptis Magna. Once a Carthaginian settlement, it later became a Roman city of eighty thousand people. It was brought to its final splendor by one of its own sons, the dark-skinned, black-bearded emperor Septimius Severus. The magnificent public baths were erected under Emperor Hadrian. (This site is explained in more detail on page 26.)

For the best examples of North African Islamic design, one must look farther west to Kairouan, once one of the holy cities of Islam in the days when the land was called Ifriqiya. The great mosque there is strictly practical, yet it is one of the most beautiful buildings. A single, huge square minaret acts as a landmark and a fortress gate through which grateful travelers can reach the sheltered enclosure inside (like the yard of the Arab caravanserai—a roadside inn where travelers can rest and recover from the day's journey). The blank outside walls give no hint of the elegant, arcaded courtyard within. The mosque itself has simple round arches that link rows of sturdy columns with just a hint of floral decoration at their tops, giving the impression of an endless forest.

Another example of a classical Greek archaeological site is Cyrene, once the home of famed doctors and the long-vanished medicinal herb silphium. Julius Caesar had 1,500 pounds (680 kg) of silphium stored away, but by the time Nero became emperor a hundred years later, only one plant could be found in Cyrene for him to use.

After the Arab invasions came the invasion of sand. Many of the marble columns of Leptis Magna were plundered by a French consul as a gift for King Louis XIV to help build the palace of Versailles. Then King George IV acquired what was left of them to make imitation ruins beside Victoria Water, an ornamental lake he had created. The bulk of the cities remained buried until the Italian invasion, when the Italian colonial government, eager to rediscover the greatness of Rome, had them excavated.

Yet the most exciting remains of Libya remain undiscovered. The ruins of Berber and Saharan towns still lie somewhere inland beneath the sweeping sands. They will have to wait because excavating teams from abroad have not been welcomed by the Libyan authorities.

Then there are the ruins of Cyrene, situated on a Cyrenaica hillside overlooking the sea. Although they are Greek in origin, the remains are far more Roman, including a forum, a theater, and baths.

BERBER

The Berber culture, which was brutally suppressed under Gaddafi, is now experiencing a revival. Today the town of Jadu has become the center for the rebirth of Amazigh culture and language. Shops have painted Amazigh signs above their doors.

Since the start of the uprising, a radio station has been broadcasting from Jadu in both Arabic and Amazigh, in what Berber activists believe are the first conversations in their language over Libyan airwaves in four decades. So far, an Amazigh publishing house has printed four books, billed as Libya's first publications in the language since Gaddafi first seized power.

The Amazigh fear that their culture may be once again undermined, as when the interim Libyan cabinet was unveiled, they found that they were, once again, left unrepresented.

INTERNET LINKS

islamic-arts.org/2011/glories-of-islamic-art
This site offers four videos showing the glories of Islamic art and architecture.

www.metmuseum.org/learn/for-educators/publications-for-educators/islamic-art-and-geometric-design
This site has activities for students that teach the principles of Islamic art.

www.scholastic.com/browse/article.jsp?id=3753881
A discussion of Islamic art and architecture can be found here.

LEISURE

Locals and tourists mix at open-air cafés in Tripoli.

11

E SPECIALLY TODAY, LIFE IS OFTEN deadly serious for most Libyans, whether they live in the desert or the city. Still, Libyans find time to take part in a wide range of sports and leisure activities.

Libyans living in the cities have no clubs or bars in which to relax. After the revolution, Gaddafi shut down night entertainment spots, which encouraged a lifestyle that contradicted strict Islamic law. Nevertheless, there are avenues for recreation in Libya. People in the cities can watch a movie in a theater or meet friends at a café. Sports, especially soccer, are

Libyans enjoy meeting with their friends over cups of tea or at a café. They also like to play cards and board games. They enjoy spectator sports such as soccer and horse racing. Hopefully with the end of the fighting, Libyans may once again take to the activities that they love.

Boys and men cool down during power outages and high temperatures in 2014.

Boys play soccer in an alleyway in 2015 in the Old City part of Tripoli.

not only leisure pursuits but have become careers for professional athletes. Horse and camel racing are also popular in the country.

Libya has many museums, most of which exhibit archaeological and Islamic artifacts. Examples are the Jamahiriya Museum of Archaeology and Prehistory in the Tripoli Castle, and the Leptis Magna Museum at Al Khums, east of Tripoli.

SPORTS

In the first years of independence, Libya hoped to show its sporting prowess in the international arena. Its Olympic debut was in 1968, when three competitors were sent to the Summer Games in Mexico City. They did not win any medals. After Gaddafi's coup in 1969, there was a very different attitude toward international relations.

At the Munich Olympics in 1972, Palestinian terrorists held several members of the Israeli team hostage and murdered eleven of them. Libya appeared to have been involved. The weapons used by the terrorists had been smuggled into Germany in Libyan diplomatic baggage. When Gaddafi hailed the five terrorists who were killed in the incident as martyr heroes, Libya was banned from participating in the Olympic Games. However, after UN sanctions were suspended in 1999, Libya took part in the Summer Games of 2000 and the Winter Games of 2002. Libya also has a team that participates in the international Special Olympic Games.

Libya's most popular sport is soccer. Matches between local teams are enthusiastically supported, and crowds often gather around a radio to listen to a broadcast. The Libyan Arab Jamahiriya Football Federation, founded in 1962, is a member of international soccer organizations.

HORSES

Horses have been a source of national pride since long before the Arabs arrived in North Africa. In 1229 BCE, an Egyptian pharaoh's soldiers captured fourteen chariots from a Libyan chief, which means that horses were being used in Libya more than three thousand years ago. We know that horse-drawn chariots were racing across the Sahara by 1000 BCE. According to the Bedouin, the queen of Sheba gave magnificent Arab stallions to King Solomon. Such horses could easily have come to her kingdom from Africa, through the regular trade route across the Red Sea.

It was the ancestors of the Libyans who introduced the Greeks to four-horse chariot racing. That was also how the Romans caught on to the idea. The Greek historian Herodotus described, in about 470 BCE, how the Garamantes, warriors from Fezzan, chased Ethiopian cave dwellers in their four-horse chariots. The Roman emperor Septimius Severus, from Libya's Leptis Magna, took Arab stallions to Britain as racehorses.

Libyans are mad about horses. There are frequently official and unofficial horse races. And the racing camel, the *mehari* (meh-HAH-ree), is also a mean contender.

The Libyan horse is one of the few natural breeds of the world, which were descended from the original wild horses of central Asia. Among the descendants of the original wild horses of Central Asia are the Spanish horse and the Arabian horse. The Greek historians Herodotus and Xenophon mention Libyan horses in their writings.

The Arabian horse is recognized as the oldest breed in the world. However, it is not certain whether it originated in Arabia as its name suggests. After the Prophet Muhammad was defeated in a battle in 625 CE because of a lack of horses, he encouraged horse breeding as a pious and religious duty.

To make sure that horses remained of totally pure pedigree, a horse's ancestry was considered sacred. If horses were captured during the constant raiding, the Arabs promptly set about checking on the pedigree of any captured mare. A messenger would be sent to the defeated side to determine this information. The information would be given, even if there was a storm of protest at the theft of so wondrous a horse.

Purebred horses were so important that in later years, Muslims were forbidden from selling Arabian horses to Christians so that the stock would remain a unique cultural treasure. Today, pure Arabian horses are some of the most distinguished breeds in the world and often win prizes at international competitions.

"I NAME THEE HORSE"

The Bedouin sing about the speed, loyalty, and beauty of Arabian horses in praise poetry. Here is a translated Bedouin praise poem:

> *When Allah willed*
> *to create the horse,*
> *He said to the South Wind,*
> *"Of thy substance*
> *shall I create a new being,*
> *for the glory of my chosen people*
> *and the shame of my enemies."*
> *And the South Wind replied,*
> *"Do thou so, Most Mighty."*
> *Then Allah took to himself*
> *a handful of wind,*
> *and breathed upon it*
> *and created a horse*
> *of red-bay color like gold,*
> *and he said, "I name thee horse."*

SCOUTS AND GIRL GUIDES

Scouting activities have spread fast in Libya since their introduction in 1954, even though Gaddafi at one point accused the Boy Scouts of America of being a front for the Central Intelligence Agency. Scouts and Guides in Libya are particularly active in the field of environmental conservation, tree-planting, and building farm roads. They also help the elderly and the disabled, visit hospitals, and undergo first-aid training. They provide more service to their own community than do Scouts and Guides in some other parts of the world.

Boy Scouts in Benghazi pack meals for rebels on the frontlines.

And, of course, they go camping. There are national Jamborees every few years, and they take part in joint activities with Scouts and Guides from other African countries. Libyan Scouts and Guides may also go to their meetings in the desert riding camels. The Libyan Scout's "promise and law" are much the same as for other Scouting associations worldwide. Their motto is *Wa A'eddou* ("Be Prepared").

Now, with the collapse of all government services in Benghazi, the 3,500 Boy Scouts of the city, most between the ages of eight and eighteen, have been cleaning the streets, distributing food and medicine, assisting doctors and orderlies in hospitals, finding homes for refugees, providing first aid to the injured, giving blood, picking vegetables, unloading aid shipments, clearing shrapnel from the airport runway, making meals for the fighters, and even cleaning the rebels' weapons. "The scouts have been brilliant. We're very proud of them. We underestimated our youth," said Iman Bugaighis, spokeswoman for the National Transitional Council.

TRADITIONAL GAMES

The Bedouin play a game that uses an eight-by-six grid of small holes in the sand. Players in turn place a pebble or bean into a hole and try to get three in a straight line. Each time a player succeeds, he or she removes one of the opponent's pebbles. There is also the game of *isseren* (IS-ser-en), which is played by throwing six split sticks into the air and scored by counting how many fall with the split side up. Chess and dominoes are also played.

TOURISM AND TRAVEL

During the 1990s, tourism in Libya was nearly nonexistent because of sanctions that prohibited civilian air travel to and from Libya. Since UN sanctions were suspended in 1999, tourism in Libya became a growing industry, with a million tourists visiting the country during the same year. With increased fighting and chaotic conditions, however, tourism to Libya has all but dried up by 2015. Most countries now advise their citizens not to travel to Libya.

INTERNET LINKS

www.thoroughbredracing.com/articles/risen-ashes-remarkable-rebirth-racing-libya
This article talks about the revival of horse racing in war-torn Libya.

www.tripolipost.com/articledetail.asp?c=17&i=9459
This site from a Libyan newspaper looks at children's games in Libya.

whc.unesco.org/en/list/183
This site takes a look at the spectacular ruins of Leptis Magna, long a tourist draw in Libya.

FESTIVALS

A young Tuareg man plays an electric guitar during the annual Ghadames Festival.

12

LIKE MOST COUNTRIES, LIBYA HAS both national and religious holidays. Libya's Islamic religious holidays, or festivals, are based on the Islamic lunar calendar, which means they occur on different days every year. The country's national holidays are fixed on the same days each year.

Libyans celebrate the third anniversary of the uprising at Martyr's Square in the capital on February 17, 2014.

The Ghadames International Festival is one of the most colorful events in Libya. It's a three-day celebration in the ancient town of Ghadames in west Libya. The event, held in October at the end of the date harvest, celebrates the heritage of the desert people. Horse and camel races are popular, along with feasting, singing, and dancing.

NATIONAL HOLIDAYS

National Day, the anniversary of the revolution, is on September 1 and is marked with speeches and parades to celebrate the start of the Jamahiriya regime. The other main national holiday is Independence Day on December 24. It celebrates the original granting of independence to the country in 1951.

Libya also celebrates national holidays on March 2, Declaration of People's Authority; June 11, Evacuation Day; and October 7, Italian Evacuation Day.

LUNAR CALENDAR

Just like many other Islamic countries in North Africa and the Middle East, Libya follows the Islamic calendar. This means that Islamic years are dated from 622 CE— the year of the Prophet Muhammad's departure from Mecca to Medina. Months are known as lunar months, each beginning with the new moon. Consequently, the Islamic year is about ten days shorter than the Western year. Islamic festivals can take place in different seasons of the year because they are held ten to twelve days earlier than in the previous year.

Libyan soldiers take part in a parade marking Independence Day.

ISLAMIC FESTIVALS

DAY OF HIJRAH (ISLAMIC NEW YEAR) When the Prophet Muhammad began preaching in Mecca, the merchants in Mecca plotted to kill him because they feared they would lose money if too many people followed his teachings. With the help of friends, Muhammad escaped into the desert and hurried north to Medina, where he knew he would be welcomed. Because this was the beginning of the first Islamic community, it is counted as the first day of the first Islamic year. It was later decided that the first day of the month of Muharram (moo-HAR-ram) should be the beginning of the Islamic year.

THE MAJOR ISLAMIC FESTIVALS

Day of Hijrah . . . . *Islamic New Year*

Tenth Muharram . . . . *Fast Day*

Milad un-Nabi. . . . . *Birthday of the Prophet Muhammad*

Lailat al-Mi'raj. . . . . *Night of Ascension*

Lailat al-Bara'ah . . . . *Night of Forgiveness*

Ramadan. . . . . *Month of Fasting*

Lailat al-Qadr . . . . *Night of Power*

Id al-Fitr . . . . *End of Ramadan*

Id al-Adha . . . . *Feast of Sacrifice*

Hijrah Day is a time when Muslims remind themselves of the stories of the Prophet Muhammad and his early companions, and they send greetings to their friends.

TENTH MUHARRAM Also known as Ashura (a-SHOO-ra), this is a day of fasting to remember Moses's success in leading the Israelites out of slavery in Egypt. Tenth Muharram is also the day the Prophet Muhammad himself kept a fast and instructed others to do the same. No weddings or forms of public entertainment take place on this day.

MILAD UN-NABI (MEE-LAD AN-NA-BEE) The birthday of the Prophet Muhammad is celebrated throughout the Islamic world. On this occasion, the birth, life, and teachings of Muhammad are recounted in readings and prayers. Libyan children usually set off firecrackers, and the evening meal includes every possible variety of dried fruit. Often the whole month of Rabi ul-Awwal, which is the third month in the Islamic calendar, is spent celebrating the Prophet Muhammad's birth and life.

LAILAT AL-MI'RAJ (LAY-LATUL-MIK-RAJ) This is the twenty-seventh day of the month of Rajab (re-JAB). On this day Muslims celebrate the Prophet Muhammad's night journey from Mecca to the bare rock of the

center of the beautiful Dome of the Rock in Jerusalem. From there, according to legend, he visited heaven on the back of his horse, Al Buraq. The rock is also believed to be the Altar of Sacrifice of Solomon's Temple. There are channels cut in the rock to carry away the blood from animal sacrifices.

LAILAT AL-BARA'AH The night of the full moon, Lailat al-Bara'ah (LAY-at ul-BAR-ah), is two weeks before the start of Ramadan. On this Night of Forgiveness, Muslims prepare for Ramadan by seeking forgiveness for old grievances against one another. Special prayers are offered, for it is believed that this night will decide a person's destiny for the coming year.

RAMADAN The month of fasting is signaled by the sighting of the new moon. All healthy adults are expected to fast through the month of Ramadan. Fasting requires Muslims to abstain from food, drink, smoking, and sex between sunrise and sunset.

Visitors to Libya during Ramadan will find themselves forced to observe the fast, whether they are Muslim or not. If they do fast all day, what they will need most at sundown is water. That is why the first meal after nightfall is often a thick, spicy soup, fruit juice, and dates.

A man prepares traditional sweet fried pastries on the first day of Ramadan.

Depending on how rich a Libyan family is, there may be more food to follow. As the family eats, they will talk and laugh and play music. In fact, nights can get rowdy. Café nightlife can go on into the early hours of the morning. Ramadan is a time of joy as well as tribulation.

It is during Ramadan that Lailat al-Qadr (LAY-latul-KAHD-er), or the Night of Power, is celebrated with readings from the Qur'an and special prayers. The mosque is full of worshippers on this day. It commemorates the occasion when the angel Gabriel revealed the Qur'an to the Prophet Muhammad for the first time.

As the month of Ramadan draws to a close, Muslims gather to watch for the new moon. When that appears, there is great rejoicing, for the festival of Id al-Fitr (Id ul-FIT-r) can begin.

ID AL-FITR After a month of fasting, this day of festivity is greeted with joy. The beginning of the day is greeted with the phrase Id Mubarak, meaning "happy feast." It is a time for a bath and new clothes, as a reminder that this should be a new beginning in peace and forgiveness. The house is specially decorated. Cards and presents are exchanged and money is given to the poor. Spicy pastries called samosas (sah-MOH-sahs) are usually served, along with a variety of sweet cakes and cookies filled with nuts, cream, and dates.

Samosas are a favorite finger food on holidays.

ID AL-ADHA The Feast of Sacrifice, or Id al-Adha (Id ul-a-DAH), is the climax of the hajj to Mecca. It commemorates the day when God stopped Abraham, called Ibrahim in the Islamic tradition, from sacrificing his son in obedience to God. Although the festival is mainly for those who have made the pilgrimage to Mecca, it is greeted with four days of rejoicing by all Muslims all over the world.

In memory of the sacrifice, it is customary for Muslim families to sacrifice a sheep on the morning of the feast day and distribute the meat to the poor. This is the time for the whole family to be together. Guests are usually invited to dinner, and greetings are sent to family and friends.

INTERNET LINKS

traveltips.usatoday.com/festivals-libya-63130.html
This website describes some of the lesser-known festivals in the Libyan desert.

www.world-guides.com/africa/north-africa/libya/libya_events.html
This site provides information about Libyan festivals in 2014 and 2015.

FOOD

A bowl of dates and cups of tea are presented on a traditional tea set.

13

W ITH LIBYA'S ECONOMY, government, and civil life in flux, getting enough food has become an increasing priority for much of the population. Libya is a major food importer, but food exporters are reluctant to trade with Libya, as they are concerned that the country will not be able to pay its bills.

FOOD SUPPLY

Libyans eat large quantities of bread and pasta, usually with a hot peppery sauce, but little meat, fresh fruit, or eggs. In the coastal regions along the Mediterranean, fruit, vegetables, wheat, and barley are grown, but these have to be supplemented by imported foods.

Libya's waters are rich with tuna, sardines, and other fish, but most of the fishing is done by Maltese, Greeks, and Italians. The local catch is not enough to meet the domestic demand, so thousands of tons of fish have to be imported every year.

One of Gaddafi's early policies discouraged small traders and replaced them with large supermarkets run by the state. The quaint Arab market, or souk, with its coffee shops and spice sellers alongside craft and leather stalls, rapidly disappeared. This policy has been changed and local produce is being encouraged once more.

Even though it is spent fasting, the month of Ramadan is a month of special food and drink enjoyed after sundown. Iftar (if-TAAr), or the breaking of the fast, is a very important time for the family to be together. Usually the women of the household spend all day cooking for the evening meal. Dates, a hot lentil soup, and tamarind juice traditionally begin the meal, but after a brief wait, larger and more substantial dishes follow.

Salads and dips of lentils and beans, sizzling grilled meats, spicy rice or couscous, and plenty of hot, flat bread are an essential part of a late-night Ramadan meal. Food is often cooked in abundance so that there is plenty for guests, family, and friends. Desserts and pastries are of special importance during the holy month, when friends and relatives stop by. It would be unthinkable not to have a plate of pastries to offer visitors along with the obligatory tea and coffee. Popular pastries include baklava (bak-LA-va), a pistachio and honey pastry with crunchy layers; basbousa (bas-BOO-sa), a semolina cake soaked in flavored syrup; and konafabilishta (ko-NAA-fa bill ish-ta), a layered pastry filled with a sweet cream center. Although the pastries can be made at home, the more popular option is to buy huge plates from the local confectioner and bring them home in parcels tied with ribbon.

During the month of Ramadan, Libyans wake up before dawn to have the last meal before sunrise, called suhur (su-HUUR). To wake people, a musician often walks through the neighborhood streets banging a small drum. Suhur is not obligatory for fasting Muslims, but it is a popular option for people who find that they work better on a full stomach. The meal is often a light fruit juice, some rice or pudding, or salad and bread. Because it is at least an hour before sunrise, most people go back to sleep until morning, so the food must be light and easy to digest. Ramadan is a month of different schedules and routines, but a time of joy and togetherness.

FORBIDDEN FOODS

Muslims all over the world have strict laws about what they may eat and drink. Alcohol is forbidden, as is pork or any food cooked in pork fat. Animals must be killed in a certain way in order for the meat to be considered *halal*, or allowed. The butcher must say a prayer three times before he kills the animal, and he must kill it in as humane a way as possible.

BEDOUIN MANNERS

A visitor will be served ground coffee or mint tea, followed perhaps by a plate of dates, before any serious conversation starts. Many families in Libya still eat in the traditional manner. The men usually eat first, while the women wait out of sight once they have served the food. The dishes are placed in the center, with the guests sitting around. No cutlery is used. Only the right hand is used. To use the left hand is considered impure, since the left hand is traditionally used for cleaning up in the bathroom.

To welcome a guest with a proper feast is a delight for the desert Bedouin. Hospitality is a strong part of Islamic custom. Even when times are difficult, a family will prepare special dishes for the guest and make sure that there is plenty of meat—an expensive commodity in Libya. The show of hospitality is a reflection on the status of the family as much as on the guests themselves.

EATING CUSTOMS

At home, Libyans eat their meals in a way that originates in Islamic custom. Before and after a meal, they say prayers. Perfumed water may be passed around. In silence, each person dips three fingers into the bowl for a ceremonial cleansing.

Before the food is served, a round of bread is placed on each plate. Food is eaten with the fingers. It is the custom for the guest to start eating first; otherwise the eldest in the family will begin. It is not common for Libyans to talk much at meal times. After the meal the hands are washed with warm water, and a prayer of thanks is said.

SPICES

Spices and herbs are essential to Arab cooking. The most common include salt, pepper, saffron, ginger, garlic, cinnamon, cumin, and coriander.

Salt is found in the Sahara Desert in deposits left by long-vanished seas. It is used as a flavoring agent, a preservative, and an antiseptic. Pepper, ground from the dried berries of the pepper vine, gives food a hot, sharp taste.

Saffron, the dried stigmas of a purple-flowered crocus, is used to flavor and color rice. It is the most expensive spice in the world. Ginger is a root that is usually dried and preserved in syrup. It gives a rich tang to meat and fruit. Garlic is a strong-smelling, medicinal herb of the onion family and is used to tenderize meat and flavor salads.

Cinnamon, a fragrant stick of bark, is ground and used as an ingredient in curry powder or in cakes and puddings. Cumin is a sharp-tasting, mildly hot seed that is used whole or powdered in curry. Coriander adds flavor and aroma to many dishes. The seed is used whole or powdered, and the leaves are added to chutneys and sauces.

BREAD AND MEAT

A woman sells *kesrah* **(flatbreads) in downtown Tripoli.**

Only foreigners in Libya eat leavened bread made with yeast. Most Libyans eat Arab breads such as *kesrah* (KES-raw), a flat pancake made of plain flour without yeast.

Considering that Libyan herdsmen tend about six million sheep, it is hardly surprising that lamb is the most common meat. It can be grilled, baked, stewed with vegetables and dates, minced or used in meatballs, and cooked on skewers as kebabs. Spit-roasted lamb is a traditional feast among the Bedouin. One popular local dish is a thick soup made with lamb stock. It contains vegetables, grains, spices, and small pieces of lamb.

Other popular dishes are *shakshouka* (shak-SHOOK-ah), chopped lamb in tomato sauce with an egg on top; *baba ghanouj* (bah-bah-ga-NOOJ), sesame seeds and eggplant made into a paste, and usually eaten with bread; and *moloukhiya* (moo-LOH-kee-ah), which is steamed vegetables with rice.

DRINKS

In a hot climate, liquid refreshment is essential. Although Libyans grow grapes, their religion forbids the drinking of wine. There are plenty of imported bottled drinks, variations on colas, and fizzy fruit juices. There is also a locally made bright-red sparkling drink called *bitter* (BIT-r) and several hot drinks prepared from ginger, cinnamon, or aniseed.

More popular are coffee and mint tea. Arabs tend to drink their coffee in small cups—thick, black, and very sweet. Mint tea is also found all over Libya as a refreshing hot (and sometimes cold) drink. Libyans are believed to drink more tea per person than people in any other country. The humblest Bedouin tent will have its copper pot brewing over coals, and hospitality demands that a visitor accept at least three glasses or cups of the fragrant, sweetened liquid.

Making tea is a time-honored ritual. The host throws a portion of green tea into a metal teapot and pours boiling water from a kettle, which may sit on its own little brazier. Sugar is added generously, followed by a bouquet of fresh mint. The lid of the teapot is closed, and conversation resumes. After the host has poured tea into his own glass, tasted and tested it, it may at last be offered to his guests and family.

INTERNET LINKS

www.food.com/topic/libyan
This site has traditional Libyan recipes from Food.com.

libyanfood.blogspot.com
Authentic Libyan recipes and photos are found here.

www.temehu.com/Libyan-food.htm
This is an article about some of the main ingredients and dishes in the Libyan diet.

SHORBA (LIBYAN SOUP)

2 tablespoons extra virgin olive oil

1 medium onion, chopped

½ pound (200 grams) boneless lamb shoulder, chopped

2 medium-size ripe tomatoes, chopped

2 Tbsp tomato paste

3 bay leaves

1 teaspoon chili powder

½ tsp cayenne pepper or harissa, or to taste

1 tsp cinnamon

1 tsp cardamom

½ tsp turmeric

Salt and freshly ground black pepper to taste

½ cup (80 g) orzo

1 cup (65 g) cooked chickpeas, drained (canned are fine)

¼ cup (5 g) fresh cilantro (optional)

½ cup (15 g) fresh parsley, chopped

1 Tbsp dried mint (don't use fresh, dried is traditional here)

1 lemon, cut into wedges

Heat oil in a large saucepan. Add onion and lamb and cook, stirring frequently, until just beginning to brown, about 5 minutes. Add tomatoes, tomato paste, bay leaves, and ground spices. Stir, then add 8 cups (2 liters) water. Bring to a simmer and cook for 45 minutes.

Add orzo and chickpeas and cook 15 minutes, until orzo is tender. Stir in cilantro, mint, and parsley. Serve with lemon wedges to squeeze over soup, and warm crispy bread.

Serves 6 to 8.

MAHALABIA (ARABIC MILK PUDDING)

3 cups (700 mililiters) whole milk
¾ cup (150 g) sugar
1 cup (240 mL) cold water
6 Tbsp cornstarch
1 cup (240 mL) heavy whipping cream
1 Tbsp rose water
2 cardamom pods, crushed

Combine milk and sugar together in a saucepan; bring to a boil.

Whisk water and cornstarch together in a bowl until smooth; stir into boiling milk. Cook milk mixture over medium heat until thickened to the consistency of cake batter, 15 to 20 minutes. Remove saucepan from heat and stir cream, rose water, and cardamom into milk mixture.

Refrigerate pudding until completely cooled, 2 to 4 hours.

Serve topped with chopped pistachios, raisins, or flaked coconut.

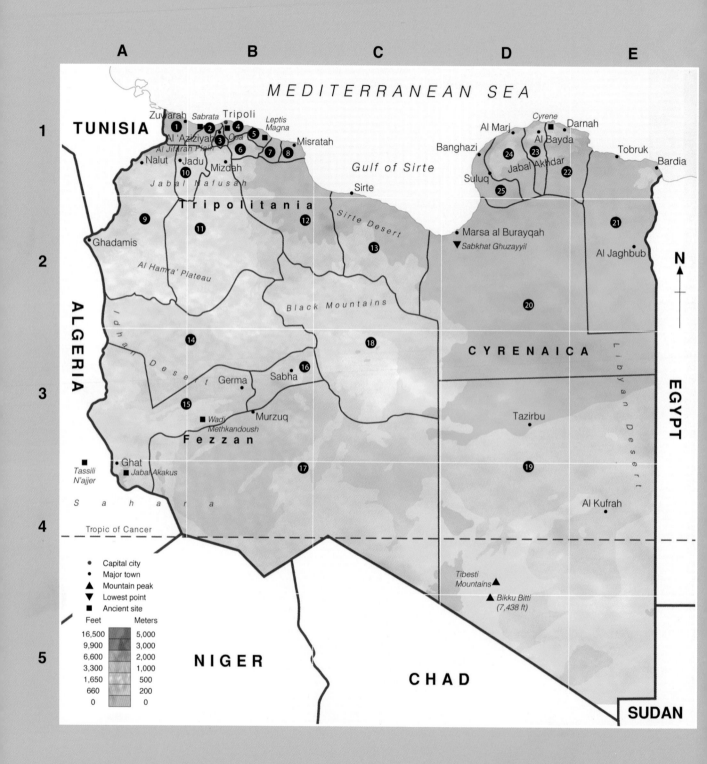

MAP OF LIBYA

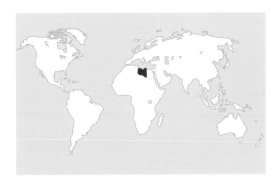

ECONOMIC LIBYA

Agriculture

 Barley

 Cattle

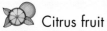 Citrus fruit

 Dates

 Olives

 Peanuts

 Soybeans

 Wheat

Services

 Airport

 Port

Natural Resources

 Natural gas

 Oil

Development Project

 Great Man-Made River

Manufacturing

 Dairy products

 Food processing

 Furniture

 Oil refining

 Textiles

 Water bottling

ABOUT THE ECONOMY

OVERVIEW

Today, as in the recent past, Libya's economy is almost entirely dependent on oil, which generates 65 percent of the country's Gross Domestic Product (GDP) and 96 percent of government revenue. Libyan sales of oil and natural gas fell apart during the revolution that overthrew Gaddafi, but rebounded in 2012 and 2013. But sales again collapsed in late 2013 and throughout 2014 as government authority collapsed across the country and rival political factions competed for control of the central bank and the national oil company and economic chaos grew.

GROSS DOMESTIC PRODUCT (GDP)

$97.58 billion (2014)

GDP PER CAPITA

$15,700 (2014)

GDP SECTORS (2014)

Agriculture, 2.0 percent; industry, 45.8 percent; services, 52.2 percent

CURRENCY

USD 1 = LYD 1.37 (2015)
1 Libyan dinar (LYD) = 1,000 dirhams

ECONOMIC GROWTH RATE

-24 percent (2014)

LABOR FORCE

1.738 million (2014)
Services: 59 percent; Industry: 23 percent; Agriculture: 18 percent

UNEMPLOYMENT RATE

32 percent (2010)

IMPORTS

Machinery, semi-finished goods, food, transportation equipment, consumer products

EXPORTS

Crude oil, refined petroleum products, natural gas, chemicals

MAIN TRADE PARTNERS

Italy, France, Germany, China, Turkey, South Korea, Egypt, Tunisia, Spain

OIL RESERVES

48.47 billion barrels (2014)

CRUDE OIL PRODUCTION

310,000 barrels/day (2014)

INDUSTRIES

Petroleum, petrochemicals, aluminum, iron and steel, food processing, textiles, handicrafts, cement

AGRICULTURAL PRODUCTS

Wheat, barley, olives, dates, citrus fruit, vegetables, peanuts, soybeans, beef

CULTURAL LIBYA

Berber hilltop village
A former desert fortress, Jadu is still an active town and a center of Berber culture, where market days and traditional festivals are a bustle of colorful activity.

Tripoli
Highlights include the old walled city (Medina), the Jamahiriya Museum with artifacts from Roman times, the arch in honor of Roman Emperor Marcus Aurelius, souks, and the Red Castle (Assai al-Hamra).

Talmitha
Also known as Ptolemais, this coastal city was a Greco-Roman trading port and storage place for products on their way across the Mediterranean Sea. The ruins excavated here include palaces, fountains, and Roman baths and statues.

Greek ruins
Cyrene, an ancient Greek colony founded in 631 BCE that later came under Roman rule, has the fountain and sanctuary of Apollo, a forum, a theater, baths, and a large second-century house.

Nalut
This town is famous for its Islamic architecture. The arches and passageways of the old bazaar and the central mosque, both more than three hundred years old, are well preserved.

Ghadames
This oasis city, known as "the pearl of the desert," is characterized by traditional desert architecture designed to provide cool relief from the desert heat.

Troglodyte dwellings
Until the last decade, the inhabitants of Gharyan lived in caves dug into the mountainside. These cave dwellings are still intact, although the dwellers have moved to more modern housing.

Ancient rock art
The Acacus Mountains are home to prehistoric rock art that goes back 10,000 years, stunning rock formations, and caves. Among the rock carvings are those of giraffes, elephants, rhinoceroses, and crocodiles.

Garamantian Civilization
Many tombs, forts, water tunnels, and mud-brick buildings can be found at the site of the Garamantian Empire in Germa and Zinchecra, supposedly inhabited by a warlike people who were skilled chariot riders.

Leptis Magna
Widely regarded as the finest Roman ruins in North Africa, the monuments here include a piazza, elaborate arches, a circus, an amphitheater, a basilica, and the famous Hadrianic baths.

ABOUT THE CULTURE

OFFICIAL NAME
Libya

NATIONAL FLAG
A crescent moon and star on a tri-band (red, black, and green) background. This flag was first used when Libya gained independence in 1951. It replaced Gaddafi's all-green flag after he was deposed.

NATIONAL SYMBOL
A black-and-gold eagle with a shield on its breast

POPULATION
6,411,776 (2015)

POPULATION GROWTH RATE
2.23 percent (2015)

LITERACY
91 percent (2015)

CAPITAL
Tripoli

OTHER MAJOR CITIES
Benghazi, Tobruk, Sirte, Musratah, Zuwarah, Darnah, Sabha, Ghadames

GOVERNMENT
Operates under two rival governments

OFFICIAL LANGUAGE
Arabic (official); English and Italian are also spoken

LIFE EXPECTANCY AT BIRTH
74.54 years for men, 78.06 years for women (2015)

GEOGRAPHICAL REGIONS
Tripolitania, Cyrenaica, Fezzan

RELIGION
Islam

ADMINISTRATIVE REGIONS
Al Butnan, Darnah, Al Jabal al Akhdar, Al Mari, Benghazi, Al Wahat, Al Kufrah, Sirt, Murzuq, Sabha, Wadi Al Hayaa, Misrata, Al Murgub, Tarabulus, Al Jfara, AzZawiyah, An Nuqat al Khams, Al Jabal al Gharbi, Nalut, Ghat, Al Jufrah, Wadi Al Shatii

ETHNIC GROUPS
Berber and Arab, 97 percent; other, 3 percent (includes Greeks, Maltese, Italians, Egyptians, Pakistanis, Turks, Indians, and Tunisians)

TIMELINE

IN LIBYA	IN THE WORLD
642 CE Arab general Amr Ibn Al-As conquers the Libyan coast for the Islamic Empire.	
909 Libya falls to the Fatimad caliphate.	**1206–1368** Genghis Khan unifies the Mongols and starts conquest of the world. At its height, the Mongol Empire under Kublai Khan stretches from China to Persia and parts of Europe and Russia.
1510 Spanish forces capture Tripoli.	
1551 Ottoman armies capture Libya.	
	1776 US Declaration of Independence
	1789–1799 The French Revolution
1911 The Italians land in Tripoli.	**1914** World War I begins.
1940 Fighting during World War II begins in the deserts of Libya and Egypt.	**1939** World War II begins.
1951 The United Nations declares Libya an independent country.	**1945** World War II ends.
1969 The September Revolution brings Colonel Muammar Gaddafi into power.	**1969** United States lands Apollo 11 spacecraft on the moon, first human walks on the moon
1992 The United Nations imposes sanctions on Libya for harboring the Lockerbie suspects.	**1997** Hong Kong is returned to China.
1999 Libya agrees to hand over the Lockerbie suspects. The United Nations suspends the sanctions, but the US trade embargo remains.	
2001 The Lockerbie trial ends. Diplomatic relations with Western governments improve.	**2001** Terrorists crash planes into New York, Washington, DC, and Pennsylvania.

IN LIBYA	IN THE WORLD
2003 The United Nations lifts sanctions on Libya.	**2003** War in Iraq begins.
	2004 Eleven Asia countries are hit by giant tsunami, killing at least 225,000 people.
2005 Libya's first auction of oil and gas exploration licenses heralds the return of US energy companies for the first time in more than twenty years.	**2005** Hurricane Katrina devastates the Gulf Coast of the United States.
2008 Italian Prime Minister Silvio Berlusconi apologizes to Libya for the damage inflicted by Italy during the colonial era and signs a $5 billion investment deal by way of compensation.	**2008** Earthquake in Sichuan, China, kills 67,000 people.
2009 Gaddafi is elected chairman of the African Union by leaders meeting in Ethiopia.	**2009** Outbreak of flu virus H1N1 around the world
2010 Russia agrees to sell Libya weapons in a deal worth $1.8 billion.	
2011 Bloody Libyan civil war lasts eight months from February to October, when Gaddafi is captured and killed. An interim government is announced later in the year.	**2011** Twin earthquake and tsunami disasters strike northeast Japan, leaving more than 14,000 dead and thousands more missing.
2012 Terrorists attack US embassy buildings in Benghazi, killing the US ambassador to Libya and three other Americans.	**2012** Barack Obama is re-elected US president.
2014 All US embassy personnel evacuated from Libya.	
2015 In September, Libya's rival factions announce a truce in an effort to fight ISIS.	**2015** ISIS expands its territory in Iraq and Syria.

GLOSSARY

Amazigh
Another term for the Berbers, who are thought to be the indigenous people of North Africa.

bayt (bait)
An extended family unit.

Bedouin
A desert nomad.

Carthage
An ancient civilization in North Africa.

Fezzan
The inland desert of Libya.

ghibli (GIB-lee)
A sandstorm.

halal
Food that Muslims are allowed to consume.

imam
The religious leader of a mosque.

kesrah (kes-RAW)
Libyan bread, made without yeast.

Kharijite
One of the sects of Islam.

Leptis Magna
The ruins of an ancient Roman city in Libya located in Al Khums, to the east of Tripoli.

Maghreb
The Berber area of North Africa, normally including Morocco, Algeria, Libya, and Tunisia.

Mehari (meh-HAH-ree)
A pedigreed racing camel.

NATO
North Atlantic Treaty Organization, a mutual defense association of European and American countries.

Oea
An ancient Roman city that occupied Tripoli's present-day location.

Phoenicians
The inhabitants of Phoenicia, an ancient region where present-day Lebanon is located.

Salaam aleikum
A traditional Arab greeting that means "peace be with you."

sheikh
The head of an Arab village or camp.

souk
A covered market with many small shops.

Tassili N'ajjer
A mountainous area of the Sahara, in Algeria near Libya's southwestern border.

Tuareg
A nomadic desert people related to the Berbers.

wadi
A dry valley that sometimes forms an oasis.

FOR FURTHER INFORMATION

BOOKS

Ham, Anthony. *Lonely Planet Libya: Country Travel Guide.* Lonely Planet. London: Lonely Planet Publications, 2011.

Harmon, Dan. *Major Muslim Nations.* Libya. Broomall, PA: Mason Quest Publishing, 2013.

John, Sir Ronald Bruce. *Libya: From Colony to Independence.* One World Short Histories. London: One World, 2008.

Kawczynski, Daniel. *Seeking Gaddafi.* Colorado Springs, CO: Dialogue Publishing Inc., 2011.

Matar, Hisham. *In the Country of Men.* New York: Dial Press Trade Paperback, 2008.

Pargeter, Allison. *The Rise and Fall of Qaddafi.* New Haven, CT: Yale University Press, 2013.

Thomas Cook Publishing. *Travelers Libya.* Peterborough, UK: Thomas Cook Publishing, 2009.

Vandewalle, Dirk. *A History of Modern Libya.* Cambridge, UK: Cambridge University Press, 2006.

Wright, John. *A History of Libya.* Columbia/Hurst. New York: Columbia University Press, 2010.

DVDS/FILMS

7 Days Libya. TravelVideoStore.com, 2010.

Cosmos Global Documentaries: *Tripolitania—Libya.* TravelVideoStore.com, 2009.

Global Treasures. *Leptis Magna Libya.* TravelVideoStore.com, 2005.

MUSIC

Arabian Delight: Music from Egypt Libya Tunisia Algeria. Abdu El-Hanid, Smithsonian Folkways, 2010.

Folk Music of the Sahara: Among the Tuareg of Libya. Hisham Mayet, 2004.

WEBSITES

BBC News Country Profiles: Libya. news.bbc.co.uk/2/hi/middle_east/country_profiles/819291.stm

CIA World Factbook Libya. www.cia.gov/library/publications/the-world-factbook/geos/ly.html

Guardian.co.uk—Libya. www.guardian.co.uk/world/libya

Library of Congress Federal Research Division Country Studies: Libya. lcweb2.loc.gov/frd/cs/lytoc.html

Libya News—Topix. www.topix.com/world/libya

Libya On Line Information and Entertainment at your fingertips. www.libyaonline.com

Libyana: Culture of Libya. www.libyana.org

Lonely Planet World Guide: Destination Libya. www.lonelyplanet.com/destinations/africa/libya

The Sabr Foundation Islam 101. www.islam101.com

UN Security Council Global Policy Forum: Libya. www.globalpolicy.org/security/sanction/libya/indxirlb.htm

BIBLIOGRAPHY

BOOKS

Ham, Anthony. *Lonely Planet Libya: Country Travel Guide*. Lonely Planet. London: Lonely Planet Publications, 2011.

Kawczynski, Daniel. *Seeking Gaddafi*. Colorado Springs, CO: Dialogue Publishing Inc., 2011.

Matar, Hisham. *In the Country of Men*. New York: Dial Press Trade Paperback, 2008.

Wright, John. *A History of Libya*. New York: Columbia University Press, 2010.

ONLINE

BBC News. Libya Country Profile. June 9, 2015. www.bbc.com/news/world-africa-13754897

_____. "Libya: The fall of Gaddafi." www.bbc.co.uk/news/world-africa-13860458

Busen, Nasser. "Libya's Endangered Wildlife." Anglo-Libyan, December 21, 2006. www.anglo-libyan.com/2006/12/libyas-endangered-animals.html

CNN. "Benghazi Consulate Attack Fast Facts." September 4, 2015. www.cnn.com/2013/09/10/world/benghazi-consulate-attack-fast-facts

Food.com. Libyan Recipes. www.food.com/recipes/libyan

Global Edge. Libya: Economy. globaledge.msu.edu/countries/libya/economy

Graff, Peter. "Ancient Language Renewed in Libyan Rebellion." *National Post*, July 11, 2011. news.nationalpost.com/2011/07/11/ancient-language-renewed-in-libyan-rebellion

International Committee of the Red Cross (ICRC). Libya: Increasing Healthcare Needs. July 5, 2011. www.icrc.org/eng/resources/documents/update/2011/libya-update-2011-07-05.htm

Islam 101. islam101.net

Islam.com. www.islam.com

Jabal al-Lughat. Linguistic Diversity in Libya. lughat.blogspot.com/2011/03/linguistic-diversity-in-libya.html

Looklex. Acasus Mountains Rock Art. looklex.com/libya/acacus04.htm

Mongabay.com. Libya—Geography. www.mongabay.com/reference/country_studies/libya/GEOGRAPHY.html

Murray, Rebecca. "A Tale of Two Governments." Al Jazeera, April 4, 2015. www.aljazeera.com/news/2015/04/libya-tale-governments-150404075631141.html

Temehu. Wildlife in the Sahara. www.temehu.com/Wild-life-in-sahara.htm

Time. "The Libyan Conflict." www.time.com/time/photogallery/0,29307,2053369,00.html

Travel Document Systems. Economy of Libya. www.traveldocs.com/ly/economy.htm

INDEX

INDEX